Thirty-four Ways
to Cast a Fly

Thirty-four Ways to Cast a Fly

by
John G. Lynde

with diagrams by Peter F. Lynde

South Brunswick and New York: A. S. Barnes and Company
London: Thomas Yoseloff Ltd

A. S. Barnes and Co., Inc.
Cranbury, New Jersey 08512

Thomas Yoseloff Ltd
108 New Bond Street
London W1Y OQX, England

SBN 498–06772–6
Printed in the United States of America

Foreword

Many fly fishermen are content with no more than two or three casts—say, overhead, roll and backhand. Others develop a more extensive repertoire by natural ingenuity or by imitation. Very few of us could name, much less describe, more than a dozen casts. Yet we may be using more than that number, in some sort of a way, every day we fish. Recognizing them for what they are and something of the mechanics behind them, can be a real help in performance.

Few people are better equipped than Mr. Lynde to undertake this intricate exposition. An outstanding caster himself and a fisherman of long experience, Mr. Lynde learned under some of the great English masters and was himself a professional teacher of flycasting for seven years. He has put this long experience to the test of some twenty years of practical use on the waters of British Columbia and the Pacific Northwest. His descriptions are clear and complete when read with the diagrammatic illustrations and fishermen should have little difficulty in following them.

One of the secrets of pleasure in fly fishing is comfort and ease under all conditions. I can think of nothing that contributes more to this than a full battery of alternative casts that the fisherman can use almost without thinking. To be able to cast effectively with trees and bush immediately behind, with the wind from any direction, at almost any force, to be able to clear a drowned line, switch direction without effort, float or drift a fly without drag—all these are essential not only to comfort but to rising and hooking fish. Any fly fisherman can learn something from this book. The casual fly fisherman or the fly fisherman of limited experience may find himself transformed into something like an expert.

The real gain to us all, though, should be an increased comfort and effectiveness on the water, a sense of mastery over the fine implements we use and the adverse elements that often beset us.

Roderick Haig-Brown
29 June 1967.   Campbell River, B.C.

Contents

Thirty-four Ways
to Cast a Fly

Trout Fly Casting

We have progressed a long way since the days when the trout fly casting pupil was told to hold a book under his arm and "punch" the rod. Thanks to great improvements in tackle and techniques, casting is now an almost effortless procedure, carried out in a relaxed position.

Nevertheless, to attain a high standard of casting proficiency requires a great deal of practice, particularly for the roll cast and the overhead cast. It is therefore hoped that the beginner will be keen enough and have enough opportunity to go out and practice twice or even three times a week until he has mastered at least these two basic casts.

It is assumed that the reader is right-handed. However, in the instructions which follow, the left-handed caster should experience little difficulty in adjusting the text to meet his requirements.

In dealing with the successive casts described, detailed explanations would obviously entail repetitions of what has already been learned in previous casts; therefore I have chosen to progress from each cast to the next instead of attempting to treat every cast individually.

Clearly the beginner would be well advised to seek tuition in such a practical art as casting from a qualified instructor rather than from any written text; but properly qualified teachers of casting are very few and far between, and instruction from a friend may be a poor substitute. On the other hand, it is hoped that this book will assist not only the beginner but also the experienced fly fisher to benefit by improving some of his techniques and adding to his repertoire of casts.

1

"Balanced" Trout Fly Tackle

With gentle movements of the wrist transmitted
and amplified through the rod, the line picks up cleanly
from the water, rises in a backward curve and extends
high in the air; then swiftly and surely the forward cast
unfolds, lengthening out and poising for a split second
before the line falls and the fly drops lightly in front of
a rising trout. There is a feeling of satisfaction in the
co-ordination of eye, hand, rod, line, leader and fly working in unity that can only be experienced when all the
related pieces of equipment are perfectly balanced.

Since a fly fisherman spends a considerable propor-
tion of his fishing time in casting, some care spent in
attaining this delicate balance would be justified if only
for the pleasure derived from casting with a well-bal-
anced outfit; but in order to achieve any degree of casting
proficiency, or even to execute some of the more skillful
casts at all, correct balance is absolutely essential.

Dealing with each item separately, first let us consider
the rod. This is the instrument that does the work, and
it should be suited to the type of fishing that it is likely
to be called upon to perform. For delicate fishing on
small streams a light rod is desirable; for big fish in
big waters where long casts are necessary, a strong rod

with plenty of backbone is required. On the other hand, the rod must suit the angler's physique.

Fly rods may be of split bamboo or synthetic materials, such as fiberglass. In my opinion good-quality split bamboo is infinitely superior to any synthetic material when used in fly rods, although the better quality glass rods are better than the cheapest bamboo rods. Synthetic rods are of tubular construction, and the strength of a tube diminishes as its bend increases simply because its circular section becomes oval under stress. Consequently tubular rods develop their maximum power at the instant of straightening, and this "snap" action is undesirable in a fly rod although it may be admirable in a spinning rod. Conversely, a split bamboo rod's power develops as the rod bends and eases as it straightens, allowing the rod to come to rest smoothly—a characteristic which is favorable to both casting a fly and setting a small hook in a fish. Moreover it is conceivable that some indefinable affinity with the angler may be present in a bamboo rod but lacking in a synthetic rod. I therefore recommend that your fly rod should be of split bamboo, or built cane, which is the same.

Rods come in all kinds of actions. Wet fly rods tend to be on the whippy side, while dry fly rods are "quicker," though not necessarily stiffer. Rods with a "tip action" are ideal for casting against a strong wind, although they require more effort and are less versatile than rods that have their actions distributed more generally throughout, such as "parabolic" rods. For general purposes some compromise is necessary, but this need not imply that an all-purpose rod will fall far short of the ideal in any circumstances likely to be encountered under normal fishing conditions. What constitutes a good all-purpose fly rod may be a matter of opinion, but the following suggestions will serve as a general guide.

Let us assume that you have decided to choose an all-purpose trout fly rod between eight and a half feet and nine feet in length, weighing approximately five or six ounces, with a fairly quick action and a curve that spreads evenly down to the butt yet is slightly more pronounced towards the tip. When waved about as in casting the rod should feel light and sensitive, and there must be no weakness at any point throughout its length. See how quickly it will come to rest; then it should be perfectly straight. Examine it thoroughly for blemishes, and check that the fittings are to your liking. Attach a fly reel, then take a loose hold of the grip and shake it rapidly from side to side so that you set up a vibration through the rod—the lower cross-over point should be near the center of the grip (Fig. 1), otherwise you might feel a "kick-back" in casting.

Pick out a number of rods which you think will suit you, even several with exactly the same specifications, and compare them all for action, feel, curve, straightness, blemishes, and vibration cross-over points. Lay aside all the rods except the two or three that have the greatest appeal to you, then compare those again until you are left with only one, which will be your final choice.

The reel plays no part in casting a fly. Its purpose is merely to store line, therefore it may be quite simple. However, certain features must be considered, such as weight, line capacity, soundness of construction, fittings and finish. The weight of a fly reel should be such that, when the reel and line are attached to your rod, the rod's point of balance will be two or three inches forward from the grip. Its line capacity must be sufficient to carry an adequate length of strong backing in addition to the fly line to meet with your fishing requirements. The reel should be sturdy, its bearings sound, and its check mechanism reliable. A contracted spool, say one inch wide, facilitates the distribution of the line on the reel. Make sure that the reel seat fits properly on your rod, other-

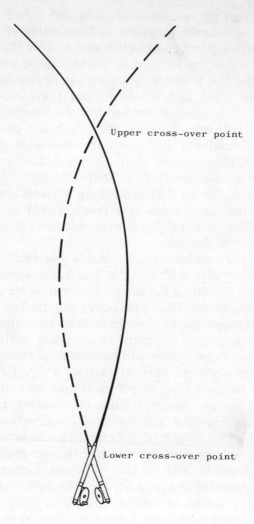

FIGURE 1. Selecting a rod.

wise it may require modification. You will probably wish to carry a floating line and a sinking line, so you may decide to acquire a spare spool with the reel; obviously a spare spool is more economical than a second reel. A quick-release catch is better than a screw to retain the spool, and a chrome line guard will protect your lines from unnecessary wear. If you expect to fly fish a lot in salt water, your reel should be anodized or corrosion-resistant.

Fly casting proficiency cannot be achieved with level lines, so we may as well discount them, but there are two entirely different kinds of tapered lines, each requiring its own technique. They are double-tapered lines and forward-tapered lines.

A double-tapered line, as its name suggests, has a long, thick level section in the center and is tapered equally at both ends; when one end becomes worn, the line can be reversed on the reel. A forward-tapered line consists of a long, thin level section, a "hinge" or back-taper, a short, thick belly, and a front taper similar to one end of a double-tapered line.

The merits of a forward-tapered line are first that the fly can be cast further than with a double-tapered line; secondly that the rod is required to lift only a relatively short length of line in order to make a long cast; thirdly that the short thick belly makes casting more effortless; and fourthly that a beginner can obtain more pleasing results with it than with a double-tapered line. On the other hand a double-tapered line is far safer to use in a cross-wind, and in my opinion more versatile. I only use a forward-tapered line for fishing when continuous long-distance overhead casting is necessary, but under such conditions it excels. I recommend that you have two double-tapered lines to suit your rod, one a floater and the other a sinker, as well as a forward-tapered line if you intend to indulge in long distance

fishing to any extent. The technique of casting a forward-
tapered line will be explained in the section devoted to
casting a long line.

The prime consideration in choosing a fly line is
whether it will balance your rod correctly. If it is too
light it will be impossible to cast properly, particularly
if there is any wind; if it is too heavy it will "kill" the
action of your rod and damage the rod. Fly lines are
made in different thicknesses to suit various rods, and
these thicknesses are usually designated by letters of the
alphabet. For example, ICH denotes a forward-tapered
line that would balance our average all-purpose fly rod,
which is 8 feet, 9 inches long and weighs between 5¼
and 5½ ounces, while HDH denotes a double-tapered
line for the same rod. The "C" and "D" refer to the
bellies of these two lines, and it would be quite in order
to use a forward-tapered line one size thicker than its
double-tapered equivalent. Most rod manufacturers spec-
ify the correct weight of line to balance a particular rod,
and line manufacturers provide a rough guide by quot-
ing the length of rod that will handle a certain thickness
of fly line. If there is any doubt as to which line will be
the right one for your rod, it is best to err on the light
side than to acquire a line that is too heavy.

Since lines play such a prominent role in fly fishing,
they must be chosen carefully. Silk may still be used
in a few of the fly lines on the market, but modern synthetic materials are superior in many ways. Dressings
are very important; they should be smooth and soft to
the touch, not wiry, yet extremely tough and durable.
Most of the cheap lines are coated with varnish, which
soon cracks and flakes off. A good line improves with use.

Having chosen your lines, see that they are firmly
spliced to the required length of strong backing when
they are put on your reels.

Surprisingly few fly fishermen are aware of the effects

which can be produced by leaders with various tapers. These tapers will enable you to cast your fly straight into the teeth of a gale, to curve your leader in either direction like a shepherd's crook, to bump and skip a bug on the surface of the water, and to drop a dry fly as delicately as thistledown. Even the most experienced angler cannot accomplish all these feats with the same leader. It is impossible to purchase leaders with anything but a "general purpose" taper at most sporting goods stores, so it will be necessary for you to make up your own tapered leaders, which can be done quickly and easily and helps your budget considerably in the long run.

First purchase small spools of limp nylon in test strengths of 3, 4, 6, 10, 15, 20 and 30 pounds. Next learn to join pieces of leader together with the blood knot, which is the strongest leader knot (Fig. 2), and how to tie a professional leader loop knot (Fig. 3). Now you are ready to start manufacturing leaders with all sorts of tapers which will be far superior to bought leaders. The basic chart below will show you how to make the

Nylon Test Strength								
Taper	3#	4#	6#	10#	15#	20#	30#	(20#)	Leader Length
General Purpose Taper	18"	20"	20"	32"	18"				9'
Fine Taper	18"	48"	24"	18"	18"				10½'
Quick Taper		18"	12"	14"	14"	14"	18"		7½'
Forward Taper			12"	12"	12"	12"	48"	16"	10½'

four different kinds of tapered leaders which are required
in order to accomplish the casts explained in this book.
Two inches should be added to each length for tying the
knots.

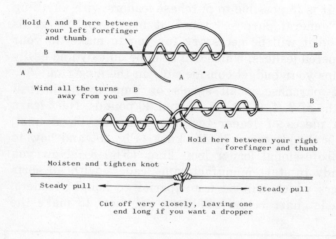

Hold A and B here between
your left forefinger
and thumb

B

A

Wind all the turns
away from you

A

Hold here between your right
forefinger and thumb

Moisten and tighten knot

Steady pull ◄───────   ───────► Steady pull

Cut off very closely, leaving one
end long if you want a dropper

FIGURE 2. The blood knot.

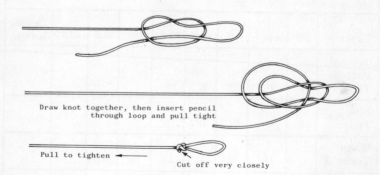

Draw knot together, then insert pencil
through loop and pull tight

Pull to tighten ◄──────

Cut off very closely

FIGURE 3. The leader loop knot.

If you are going to use a very light rod and a fine HEH line, this chart should be scaled down accordingly by substituting the top row of figures referring to test strengths as follows: "2#, 3 , 4#, 6#, 10#, 15#, 20 #. (15#)." You can, of course, vary the tapers to suit yourself, but this can only be done with experience.

The general purpose taper is what its name implies, it forms a properly balanced leader for most of the simple, straightforward casts. The fine taper is for dropping the fly lightly, casting a slack line, and casting a negative curve. The quick taper will always tend to fly out straight, even against a wind. The forward taper will develop a cow's tail action which is used to cast a positive curve or to bounce a fly on the water.

Let us assume you are waiting to make up some general purpose tapered leaders. The easiest way is to make them in pairs. Begin with 40 inches of 15 pound test nylon (twice 18 inches plus twice 2 inches for knotting both ends). Tie a loop knot at each end and slip both the loops over a convenient hook. Pull the middle towards you and cut it. Join each end of a 68 inch piece of 10 pound test nylon (twice 32 inches plus twice 2 inches) with a blood knot to each of the cut ends hanging from the hook, then pull the middle towards you and cut. Repeat this procedure with 44 inches of 6 pound test, 44 inches of 4 pound test and 40 inches of 3 pound test nylon. Now your two leaders are ready to be coiled and stored in your tackle box.

Your fly casting equipment will be completed by the addition of a small assortment of flies, which should have the hooks cut off at the bend as a safety precaution. For further protection you would be wise to wear a hat during your practice casting sessions. A piece of wool may be used to substitute the fly, but more satisfactory results will be obtained by using actual flies. When you lose a fly, replace it immediately, because without it your leader will crack like the end of a whip, and it will soon be ruined. Always practice with a leader and fly attached to your line.

Having acquired a properly balanced outfit, you will no doubt want to take good care of it; in conclusion, a few words of advice may perhaps be helpful:

(1) Never put away rods in a damp case. After fishing dry your rod with a cloth and hang it up in a dry, airy place for safe storage, with stoppers in the ferrules.

(2) Never leave your rod for long in an aluminum travelling container.

(3) When setting up or dismantling your rod, always grasp the ferrules, not the cane. Suction joints should be lined up and pushed straight in or pulled straight out, not twisted.

(4) Generally a rod bag is made to hang up by the opposite end from the opening; therefore the tip end of each rod section should be inserted first into its compartment in the bag, so that the butt ends will be at the bottom when hung up.

(5) Now and then, and particularly after each season's fishing, rods should be examined for defects, and, if necessary, repaired. Chips in the varnish should be touched up with rod varnish, damaged guides replaced (a damaged guide can spoil a line very quickly), and worn tyings renewed and varnished.

(6) Your reel needs very little attention, but it should be taken apart, wiped clean and lubricated occasionally; it is particularly important to attend to this as soon as possible after exposure to wet weather or immersion.

(7) Although most synthetic lines are rot-proof, it is always best to strip the wet portion of your line

off your reel after use, leaving it to dry in loose coils on newspaper or on a line dryer, otherwise it might corrode the reel.

(8) Nylon leaders and leader material should be kept in a dark place, otherwise they will weaken or rot. Leaders should be tested by a steady pull at intervals while fishing, and the tippets (points) replaced when weak.

2

The Roll Cast

The overhead cast and the roll cast are the two basic casts from which all the others are derived. Both must be mastered before further progress can be expected, yet once you have learned to accomplish them successfully you should experience no difficulty with the remaining trout fly casts included in this book, nor indeed with any that may have been omitted.

Do not expect to become an expert overnight. You will probably need many hours of arduous practice to learn just the two basic casts. All this must be done on water, so try to find an open pool or a stream with a clear bank. If you can persuade another fly fisherman to go along with you on your casting expeditions, get him to criticize your mistakes and help you to correct them. He will be able to watch you and tell you what you are doing wrong. Do not make your sessions too long. One hour is sufficient, and little will be gained by prolonging them.

Having arrived at the water you are ready to tackle up. At first you will be using your double-tapered floating line. Fix the reel firmly on your rod and thread the line through all the guides, making sure that none are missed. Attach a general purpose tapered leader to the line by means of a figure eight knot (Fig. 4), and tie on one of your practice flies with a turle knot (Fig. 5).

FIGURE 4. The figure 8 knot.

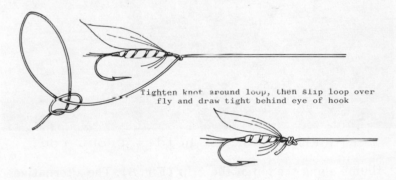

Tighten knot around loop, then slip loop over
fly and draw tight behind eye of hook

FIGURE 5. The turle knot.

Move into position for casting, and pull some line from
the reel, so that you have about fifteen feet of line and
leader hanging free from the rod tip. Hold the leader in
your left hand so that the fly is just clear of the ground.

There are several ways in which you can hold the rod.
It is helpful to know two, so that if your rod hand becomes
sore or uncomfortable you can ease it by changing from
one hold to the other. For the first, hold the grip of the
rod firmly *in the fingers* of the right hand, and place your

FIGURE 6. How to hold a trout rod.

thumb along the top of the grip (Fig. 6). The alternative
hold is made by placing the rod diagonally across the
palm of the right hand and tightening the fingers, placing the thumb firmly along the left side of the grip, so
that the first knuckle of the forefinger is above the grip
(Fig. 7).

Now you are ready to begin casting. Stand comfortably
with your feet a few inches apart, facing half right.
Wave your rod back, then flick it forward, simultaneously
releasing the leader from your left hand. It does not matter if the line falls in a heap in the water; the roll cast,
if you do it correctly, will pick it up easily.

The roll cast comprises three distinct movements. First
raise your rod to sixty degrees by raising your forearm

FIGURE 7. Alternative hold.

from the elbow (Fig. 8). Secondly, maintaining your shoulder, arm and rod in this position, swing your body to the right, so that the rod tip, still pointing upwards at sixty degrees, also swings through a quarter-circle (Fig. 9); continue the rod-swing, raising your forearm until your right hand is almost touching your shoulder with the rod pointing up and to your right. Thirdly, swing your body to the left, and with an impulse from your shoulder throw your right hand towards where you wish to place your fly, at the same time forcing your hand down smartly from the wrist with a hammer-blow action so that your rod point comes to rest a few inches above the surface of the water (Fig. 10). The rod's plane should

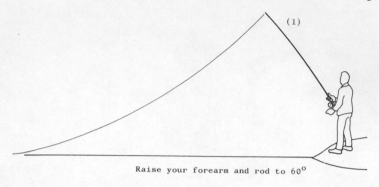

Raise your forearm and rod to 60°

FIGURE 8. The first phase of the roll cast.

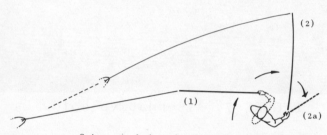

Swing your body and rod to the right, dragging
the leader and fly on the water

FIGURE 9. Plan of the second phase.

be vertical for the forward cast. If you allow two sec-
onds for each phase of the roll cast, your timing will be
about right for the short length of line you are using. In
order to co-ordinate your movements with this timing,
try saying to yourself "one-hundred-thousand, two-hundred-thousand, three-hundred-thousand."

Plan of the forward cast

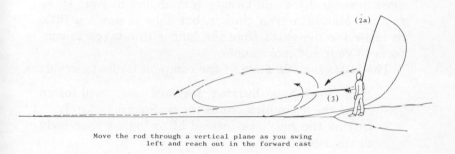

Move the rod through a vertical plane as you swing
left and reach out in the forward cast

FIGURE 10. The third phase.

In theory the roll cast is very simple. The first phase
starts the line moving and lifts most of it clear of the
water. The second phase swings the line outwards to your
right side, and, with the fly anchored to the water, a "D"
begins to form as shown in Figure 10. The third phase
throws the "D" forwards into a loop with sufficient momentum to straighten out and carry the fly to the full extent of the line.

Practice these movements with their correct timing
until you are confident of your co-ordination and are
achieving at least a majority of perfect roll casts. You
can prevent your line from lengthening by curling your
forefinger around it in front of the reel and holding it
against the rod grip. At first you may meet with little
success in your casting efforts, but occasionally you will
be pleased to discover that you have accomplished a good

cast; when this occurs, try to find out what you did that was different, then endeavor to repeat it. When you are sure you have mastered the short length of line with which you began, strip another five feet of line from your reel with the left hand and help it to run out through the guides by waving the rod gently over the water. Then continue practicing until you have managed to control the full twenty feet of line to your satisfaction. Maintain even timing, but slow it down a little to allow for the extra time the longer line takes to conform to your rod movements.

The following are some of the common faults to avoid:

1. Poor timing—a hurried forward cast will often cause the fly to flick out of the water prematurely.
2. Lifting the rod back instead of swinging your body to the right.
3. Failure to raise your rod to a vertical position at the end of the sideways swing.
4. Failure to deliver sufficient power to your forward cast.
5. Failure to follow through in your forward cast so that your rod stops just above the water.
6. Aiming too low—raise the imaginary nail at which your hammer-blow is directed.
7. Hesitation or jerky movements—try to make your casts as smooth and rhythmical as possible.

Now that you are able to roll cast twenty feet of line with reasonable assurance, you may begin to wonder how to lengthen the line still more. This is where your left hand comes into action. Release the line from your right forefinger and grip it just in front of the reel between your left thumb and forefinger. As you raise the rod in the first phase of the roll cast, straighten your left arm and reach back with your hand, pulling line off the reel and in through the rod guides (Fig. 11). Keep your left

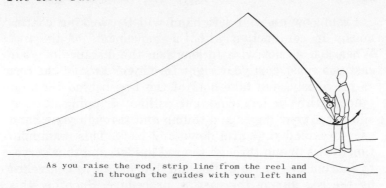

As you raise the rod, strip line from the reel and
in through the guides with your left hand

FIGURE 11.   Lengthening line.

hand in this position through the second phase and when
your rod is about half way through its forward arc in
the third phase, swing your left arm forwards in a bowling action toward the first guide of your rod and release
the line (Fig. 12). Do not be disappointed if the line fails
to "shoot" the first time, as it takes quite a lot of practice to achieve complete co-ordination and perfect timing.

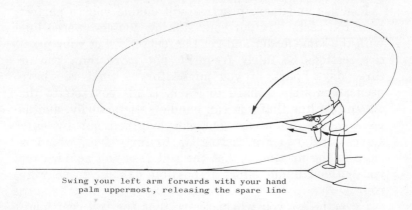

Swing your left arm forwards with your hand
palm uppermost, releasing the spare line

FIGURE 12.   "Shooting" line.

From now on your left hand will be working continuously in conjunction with the movements of the rod. When you do not wish to lengthen the distance of your cast you must curl your right forefinger around the line as previously, and take hold of the line behind the first guide with your left hand, but without gripping it, let it slide over your finger and thumb and through your hand as you extend your arm down and back. This manipulation draws line in through the rod guides, and thus serves to shorten the length of the line that has to be controlled by the rod during the casting procedure. Shooting this spare line also contributes to the smoothness of line "run out" in the forward cast.

It is important to keep your left elbow straight and your arm extended well back until the moment of shooting line, otherwise your left hand would be holding the line at an angle away from the rod and some power would be lost during the forward cast. This is because the rod would approach your hand on its downward movement, allowing the resulting slack line to slip through the guides and escape at the very instant when the rod should be pulling the "D" forwards.

Practice and more practice will enable you to perfect your roll casts. Try out your sinking double-tapered line with the same leader and get the feel of it. Let your practice sessions be fairly frequent, not more than two or three days apart, or you might forget what you have been struggling so hard to learn. Limit yourself to the amount of line that you can handle satisfactorily, and as your casting improves you can lengthen out by easy stages until you are casting up to forty feet, which is close to the maximum that the roll cast will achieve for you without undue effort or possible damage to your fly rod.

Nevertheless you will perceive that the roll cast itself has some value. With a wind blowing from behind it is the easiest, laziest cast to perform, for the wind will help to carry your line and fly straight out in front of you. Moreover, if two fly fishers are fishing in the same direction from a boat, the angler on the left can avoid endangering or interfering with the angler on his right by using the roll cast, which will keep the fly always in front of him and at a safe distance from the boat. However, the most useful aspect of the roll cast is its ability to free the line from the water. Hence it is often combined with other casts which are not so well blessed with this characteristic.

3

Overhead Casting

Of all the casts that have ever been invented the overhead cast is by far the most commonly used. Properly carried out it is a clean cast, pleasing to perform and beautiful to behold. With it the fly can be placed with great accuracy at all distances.

You will be using exactly the same tackle combination as you used for learning the roll cast, so put your rod, reel and double-tapered floating line together, and attach a general purpose tapered leader and fly.

Stand facing half right near the water's edge with your feet a little apart, and hold the rod by either of the two methods described in the previous chapter. Since you can now accomplish the roll cast, use that to place about twenty feet of straight line on the water.

At this stage you will have so much to think about that it will be better to give your left hand a rest while you concentrate on what your right hand is doing. Hold the line with your right forefinger so that it cannot be pulled off the reel.

There are four phases in the overhead cast, and they consist of a slow raise of the rod, a back cast, a forward cast, and a follow through, carried out in equal timing. So, starting at the beginning, and referring to a clock face for angles, raise your forearm and rod from the elbow to ten-thirty; then, without checking or hesitating, continue into the second phase by moving the rod rapidly to twelve o'clock, but tilt it a little to the right by pointing your forearm in that direction. This second phase movement originates from the shoulder and is simultaneously amplified by the elbow and wrist, yet your whole body and arm should be relaxed as in throwing a small pebble. Pause in the twelve o'clock position to allow the line to extend behind you, then make the forward cast to ten o'clock with a hammer-blow action at an imaginary nail in an imaginary wall; steady your rod by tensing your hold on the grip for a split second, and, without checking, follow through by lowering your forearm and rod, keeping the rod tip more or less level with the line as it extends in front of you, and stopping it a foot above the water at about eight o'clock. (Figures 13 and 14 show all four phases.)

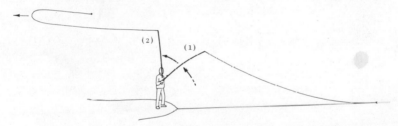

FIGURE 13. The back cast.

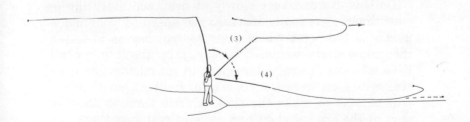

FIGURE 14. The forward cast.

Too complicated? Not if you analyze and battle through the phases one by one. When you have done that, try to achieve smoothness by acceleration and deceleration instead of sudden jerks. Compare the movements of the backward and forward casts to those of a pendulum, slow-fast-slow, slow-fast-slow.

There is a very simple exercise with a walking stick, folded umbrella or similar article. Hold it as though it were a fly rod, and move it back and forth carefully through an arc (Fig. 15).

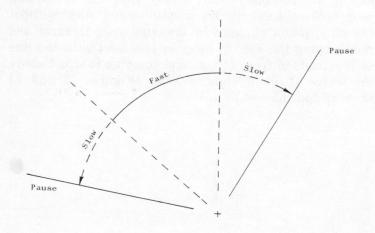

FIGURE 15.   Stick exercise.

Do this exercise very slowly at first, concentrating on smoothness; gradually increase the speed of your movements to the point where your control begins to lessen, then slow down to where you regain absolute control. Five minutes of every day spent in practicing this exercise will soon improve your co-ordination, so that you will be able to make the stick whistle through the fast part of the arc yet start and come to rest smoothly.

Now apply exactly the same principles to fly casting,

picking up your line cleanly and accelerating into the back cast as the fly leaves the water, also allowing your rod to drift or follow through to one o'clock after each back cast. This will cause your line to extend more smoothly behind and give you a wider angle for the third phase, or power movement of your forward cast.

Practice as often as you can, but confine your sessions to about one hour. Every time your line falls in a heap, use the roll cast to straighten it out and immediately make your next overhead cast. This extremely useful trick is known as *the roll pick up*. Stick rigidly to the timing, which is a slow, even "One-and-*two*-and-*three*-and-four" (the second and third phases are italicized because they are the power movements). You will probably discover quickly that whenever your back cast is a success your forward cast shows good results too. There is no need to worry about your line falling to the ground while you pause after the back-cast, so long as your back cast does the job; turn your head around and watch it during the pause if you like.

Now for a formidable list of faults commonly committed in the overhead cast:

1. *Timing too hurried or uneven.* "Whip cracking" behind denotes a too-hurried forward cast or a weak back cast.
2. *Moving your rod too far back in the second phase.* The rod movement must be slowed down before the rod passes twelve o'clock, although drift beyond that point is in order. The remedy is to watch your rod in the back cast and check it at the right instant. The use of the alternative hold (Fig. 7) sometimes cures this fault effectively.
3. *Rough pick up.* This will ruin your back cast. Time the first and second phases so that the line picks up smoothly and cleanly and the fly is leaving the water as you begin to accelerate into the back cast.

4. *Thrashing the line.* Excessive power arcs are a waste of energy, besides causing a wide loop, or entry (Figs. 13 and 14). Narrow entries are obtained by restricting the power movements to their correct arcs.

5. *Insufficient power.* If the line fails to extend fully behind or in front of you, even with a narrow entry, add a little more "flick" to the appropriate rod movement.

6. *Rod creeping forwards during pause.* This causes your back cast to bounce forwards instead of being fully extended when you begin the forward movement, and results in a jerky forward cast with little control.

7. *Jerky movements.* Casting must be smooth and easy throughout.

8. *Casting too high or too low.* First ensure that your line entries are narrow, both behind and in front. Then correct a cast that is too high by adjusting your arc of power slightly forward, so that your back cast has more lift and your forward cast will be lower. A cast that is too low can be corrected in the opposite manner by adjusting your arc of power slightly back. Under normal conditions the line should extend horizontally behind and in front.

9. *Failure to follow through after the forward cast.*

10. *"Hooking" or "Slicing."* Loss of power and direction will be caused by the rod deviating from its plane of movement. Avoid any tendency to swing the rod to either side of this plane while the back cast or forward cast is in progress, although each may be carried out in its own plane.

11. *Leader fouling up in the air.* An excessively narrow entry will cause this, and the remedy is to widen your entries by increasing your arcs of power and following through properly. Another possible cause is an incorrectly tapered leader.

12. *Line or fly fouling the rod or striking your head.*
Tilt your forearm and rod further to the right,
and avoid jerky movements.

No doubt it will have taken considerable time, effort
and patience to overcome all the problems encountered
in casting a relatively short line of twenty feet. Unfortunately there are still more troubles ahead of you when
you begin to manipulate the line with your left hand as
in the roll cast; but you have come through that experience once, so co-ordination will be easier this time. Are
you ready to give it a try?

Grip the line in front of the reel between your left forefinger and thumb. While you raise your rod in the first
phase of the overhead cast, strip line off the reel and in
through the rod guides by extending your left arm and
hand well back. This will facilitate your pick up. So far,
so good. It is exactly what you did in the roll cast. Now
you must keep your arm and hand extended behind your
left hip while you complete the second and third phases.
Early in the follow-through, while your line is beginning
to move forwards with its narrow entry (Fig. 14), bring
your left hand forwards towards the first guide with an
underarm bowling action, palm uppermost, and open your
finger and thumb to shoot the line. When you can perfect
the timing, the line will fly from your hand very smoothly
and easily. To accomplish this feat, substitute your "One-
and-*two*-and-*three*-and-four" timing with "Left-hand-
right-hand-*right*-hand-left," although you will find that
the shoot must take place a fraction of a second before
the final "left."

Be careful not to release the line too early, which
would sap the power of your forward cast as well as cause
a jerk. Put a little more drive into your back cast and forward cast in order to add enough momentum to pull out
the slack line from your left hand. Finally, cast suffi-

ciently high to allow the shoot to be completed before the line touches the water.

Control the length of your line as in roll casting. When you do not wish to increase your casting distance, curl your right forefinger over the line and manipulate your left hand from close behind the first guide with the loose sliding hold of the line that was explained in the previous chapter. Never try to cast more line than you can manage satisfactorily; and when the line fails to pick up easily, resort to the roll pick up. When your line is shooting successfully at every cast, and you can cast up to forty-five feet with complete assurance, you may proceed with the next step.

There are various ways of retrieving line while fishing. Gathering it in loose coils with your left hand is the simplest. Begin by laying out a cast of forty-five feet. Grip the line behind the first guide with your left forefinger and thumb, and strip line in through the guides as before. Curl your right forefinger over the line that you have stripped in (Fig. 16). Still gripping the line with your left hand, move your left hand forwards and take a second grip of the line just behind your right forefinger. Loosen the hold of your right forefinger while you again strip line in with your left hand and arm. You will now be holding a coil of line in your left hand (Fig. 16). Extend your left arm and hand well back as before as you raise the rod for the pick up, and shoot the coil of line during the fourth phase of your cast in precisely the same manner as previously. Having mastered the process, you can now cast a longer line with the overhead cast by stripping several feet of line from your reel before starting to retrieve. Holding three or four coils of line in your left hand, make a powerful enough cast to shoot all the coils. If you have more coils of slack line in your left hand than you can shoot, release two or three coils in a preliminary cast, then pick up immediately and cast again, shooting

FIGURE 16. Retrieving line in coils.

the remaining line. I would reiterate, "Do not try to cast a longer line than you can handle." A cast of sixty feet is ample with a double-tapered line.

Fishing a˙dry fly entails false casting, which is the process of drying the line and fly in the air between casts. In addition, false casting facilitates speed in lengthening your casts, and assists in the accurate placing of the fly; therefore it is also frequently used in wet fly fishing to get the line out to an appreciable distance. It is carried out by repeating the two power phases of the overhead cast.

Begin with a relatively short line of thirty feet. Raise your rod in the first phase, simultaneously stripping in a few feet of line with your left hand in a single movement as explained earlier. Complete the back cast, phase two, and the forward cast, phase three, retaining the line in your left hand and keeping your left arm still behind your hip. Instead of following through, as soon as the line has extended in the air after the forward cast, make another back cast and another forward cast, then a third back cast and forward cast. This time shoot your line and follow through in the fourth phase. Summarizing the whole procedure we have the following movements to carry out: raise and strip, first back cast, first forward cast, second back cast, second forward cast, third back cast, third forward cast, shoot and follow through, all done in equal timing.

False casting should be done vigorously in order to dry the line and fly, but without undue effort. Put the same amount of energy into your false casts as you put into your final cast, and avoid any tendency to bend your body forward in a stooping position after your final cast. Practice until you can handle forty or fifty feet of line in the air, limiting yourself to two false casts and a final cast as a general rule, and always aiming your false casts high so that they will not touch the water. Maintain narrow entries and keep the line moving fast.

Now you can apply your false casting technique to the task of getting your line out. Begin with fifteen feet of line and leader hanging free from the rod and a few feet of slack between the reel and the first guide. Hold the leader in your left hand, so that the fly is just clear of the ground. Wave your rod back, then flick it forwards in a false cast, simultaneously releasing the leader from your left hand and allowing the slack line to be pulled through the guides. As you begin your first back cast, seize the line in front of the reel with your left hand and strip line from the reel. Shoot this after your next false cast while the line is extending in the air, but maintain a loose hold of the line. Strip more line from your reel during your next back cast and repeat the process until you have enough line in the air to make your final cast and shoot. Three or four false casts made in this manner should suffice to give you adequate distance.

Your false casts will help you achieve accuracy with the fly by gauging both direction and distance, so make your practice session more interesting by aiming your fly successively at different objects floating on the surface. You will be surprised to discover how difficult it is to place your fly right on target!

There is just one more thing to learn about the overhead cast, and that is how to do it in conjunction with *the switch pick up*. The switch pick up can only be used to free a relatively short line from the water, but it does this with far less disturbance than the roll pick up and is very easy. First hold your rod on its right side pointing along the line so that the palm of your right hand is uppermost. Secondly, raise your forearm and rod slowly and swing the rod a little to your right. Thirdly, give your rod a smart flick horizontally or slightly upwards towards the left, then immediately start to make a normal overhead back cast. The line, leader and fly will spiral neatly into the air before their backward journey, leaving scarcely a dimple on the surface of the water.

Substitute your floating line with your double-tapered sinking line and the same leader, and go through the whole rigmarole again: the simple wet fly cast, the roll pick up, the switch pick up, retrieving your line in loose coils and shooting it from the coils, and getting your line out by false casting.

Now you have mastered the overhead cast with all its intricacies. You can use it with the roll pick up and with the switch pick up. You can regulate the length of the line quickly and achieve extreme accuracy by false casting. It was worth the struggle, for the overhead cast will stand you in very good stead.

4

Techniques of Slack Line Casting

Casting a Slack Line

In the earlier stages of learning the roll and the overhead casts, you probably experienced considerable difficulty in making nice straight casts. But try to cast a slack line now and the odds are favorable that it will fly out beautifully straight. There are occasions, particularly in fishing a stream, when a slack line is required, and this can be accomplished by four separate methods or by a combination of those methods.

The effects of casting a slack line will be enhanced if you use your floating line with one of the fine tapered leaders described in the first chapter instead of the general purpose tapered leader which you have used hitherto. All four methods work very nicely in conjunction with the overhead cast.

The first and easiest method is to check your rod at the top of the follow-through so that your line extends fully in front of you then bounces back before falling on the water (Fig. 17). Once the line has fully extended and started to bounce back, make a normal follow through to the eight o'clock position. Of course you will not be able to shoot very much line if you want a strong bounce back. Using this method will result in your line assuming a big irregular "S" bend as it falls.

FIGURE 17.   Checking before following through.

The second method, which has much the same effect as the first, is to pull back a little line with your left hand following the shoot. When used in combination with the first method the results are exaggerated in accordance with the strength of the bounce back.

The third method is to begin shooting the line just before the forward power cast has been completed. Its effect is erratic, with the line falling in irregular curves.

The fourth method, which is ineffective in a wind, is to aim the forward cast very high in the air (Fig. 18). After the line has extended it will fall to the surface in a great number of small loops, most pronounced near the fly. The third and fourth methods may be used in combination to obtain exaggerated effects.

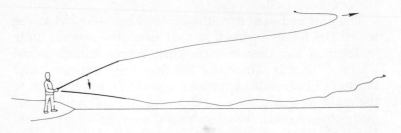

FIGURE 18. The high forward cast.

"Mending" the Line

Since the purpose of this maneuver is to prevent the fly dragging, by counteracting the action of a current upon the line, it is best practiced on a stream if at all possible. Choose a location where the current is fast near your own bank, with slower water about thirty feet across the stream.

Still using your double-tapered floating line and a fine tapered leader, make a straight overhead cast into the slow water and observe what happens. The fast current will pull your line downstream in a loop, and the fly will follow it, dragging downstream very rapidly (Fig. 19).

In order to overcome this problem, cast a slack line to (1). By the time the fly has drifted to (2), a belly will have begun to form in the line, and it should be "mended" to the left. When the fly has reached (3), "mend" the line again, then allow the line to swing around through (4), fishing the fly across the stream through (5).

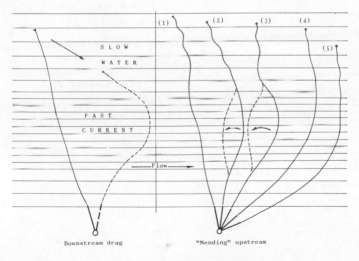

FIGURE 19. Correcting downstream drag.

"Mending" the line under these circumstances is accomplished by raising your right arm and rod horizontally outwards across the stream, lifting part of the line clear from the surface of the water, and swinging it towards the left with a gentle sweeping motion. There must be no attempt to flick the line to the left, otherwise the fly will be jerked from its position; a "mend" should not interfere with the natural downstream drift of the fly.

A different situation will arise when you are fishing the fly in a fast current on the other side of a back eddy or relatively slow water (Fig. 20). This time the drift of the fly is impeded by the line, which is held by the slow water, so a slack line should be cast to (1), and "mended" to the right at (2), (3), and (4) by the method already described.

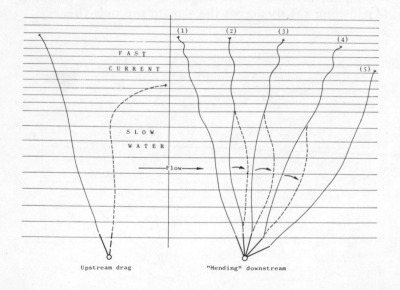

Upstream drag   "Mending" downstream

FIGURE 20.   Correcting upstream drag.

Casting a "Mended" Line

It is a lot easier to cast a "mended" line than might be supposed, and of course this will save having to make the first "mend" on water.

If you wish to make a "mend" to the left in the air, make an overhead cast, but during the forward power movement roll your wrist to the left and back again so that the rod leaves its plane and returns to it before the follow through. An early wrist roll will place a curve in the line near the leader, and a later one will place a curve nearer to the rod (Fig. 21). With a little practice you will be able to adjust your timing so that the curve will be exactly where you want it. Casting a "mended" line to the right is accomplished in the same manner, but with a wrist roll to the right and back to the normal position.

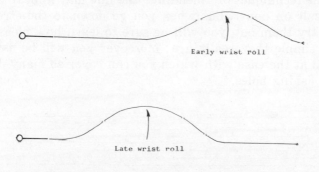

Early wrist roll

Late wrist roll

FIGURE 21. Casting a "mended" line.

Now you may wish to drift your fly through some slow water beyond a band of fast current (Fig. 22). Using an early wrist roll, cast a "mended" line to (1), "mend" upstream at (2), mend downstream at (3), and fish the fly across through (4). Conversely, if you wish to drift your fly down a fast current across a band of slack water (Fig. 23), cast a "mended" line to (1) with the loop to the

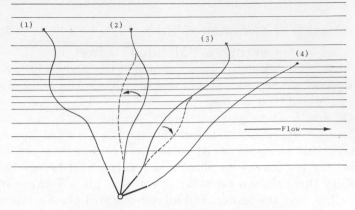

FIGURE 22. Across a band of fast current.

right near the leader, "mend" downstream at (2), "mend" upstream at (3), and fish your fly across through (4).

The techniques of "mending" the line may appear very difficult on paper, but when you go down to the stream and try them out, you will be sure to learn how pleasant and simple they really are; moreover you will be astonished at the ease with which you can cover so many difficult fishing holes.

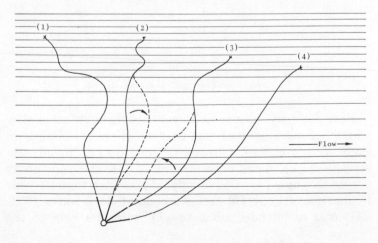

FIGURE 23. Across a band of slack water.

5

Spey Casting

The Spey Cast

The Spey cast is a derivative of the roll cast. Although the roll cast is complete in itself, it does not readily allow a change of direction, whereas the Spey cast is a true change-direction cast. Moreover the Spey cast is more clean cut, more decisive, and more sophisticated. Originally evolved for salmon fly fishing on the River Spey in Scotland, its primary purpose is to pick up a fly from downstream and cast it across; but it may also be used in fishing from a boat or in any circumstances where the roll cast might be useful. It is particularly easy to perform when the wind is from behind. Since in Spey casting the fly never goes behind the angler, it is the most practical way to fish a stream when wading in front of a heavily bushed bank.

For learning and practicing both the Spey and double Spey casts, use your double-tapered sinking line and a general purpose tapered leader. If possible, choose a stream where you can wade in shallow water and have the current flowing from right to left. Stand so that you are facing across the stream.

Lay out about thirty feet of line with a roll cast or overhead cast and allow the stream to drift your line around to the left. If you have to practice on still water, cast about forty-five degrees left from the direction in which you intend to Spey cast.

The first phase of the Spey cast is the same as that of the roll; raise your rod to an angle of sixty degrees (eleven o'clock). In the second phase, swing your body to the right, but roll your wrist a little to the right (don't flick), so that the point of the rod dips slightly as you swing, causing the line and fly to leave the water momentarily and to swing outwards by centrifugal force

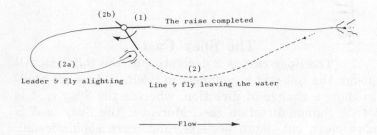

FIGURE 24. Plan of the swing.

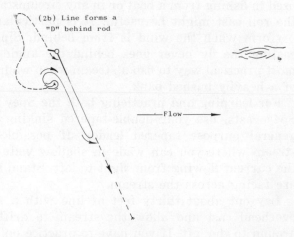

FIGURE 25. Plan of the forward cast.

until the leader and fly come to rest on the water in front of you (Figs. 24 and 27). Most of the line should now form a "D" in the air behind your rod, with the leader and fly anchored to the water, as in the roll cast explained in an earlier section. Continue with the rod swing, raising your forearm until your right hand is close to your shoulder with the rod pointing upwards and slightly back. In the third phase, swing your body to the front as you throw your arm and rod into a pointing position at the spot where you wish to cast your fly (Figs. 25 and 28), then lower your arm and rod in the follow through. You will find out in practice that the forward cast should be begun just after the leader and fly touch the water, not after they have come to rest.

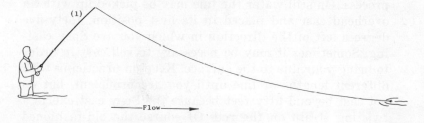

FIGURE 26. The raise completed.

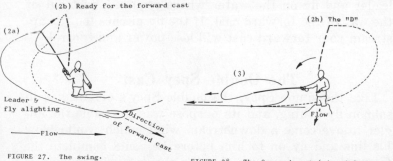

(2b) Ready for the forward cast

(2a)

(2h) The "D"

Leader &
fly alighting

Direction
of forward cast

(3)

Leader &
fly alighting

Flow

Flow

FIGURE 27. The swing.

FIGURE 28. The forward cast (viewed from downstream).

Timing of the three phases of the Spey cast is similar to that of the roll: "One-hundred-thousand, two-hundred-thousand, three-hundred-thousand." It is to be assumed that since you have fully mastered both the roll cast and the overhead cast, you will experience no difficulties in controlling and shooting the line with your left hand, the shoot taking place a little before the rod finishes its forward arc. Whereas in the original Spey the forward cast was a "thrash down," it is just as easy to make your forward cast in the air by the method just described, and the result is a much cleaner cast.

Having completed your first Spey cast, allow the line and fly to swing around in the stream, or to save time cast downstream with an overhead cast, then repeat the process. On still water the line may be picked up with an overhead cast and placed in its first position, forty-five degrees left of the direction in which you are Spey casting. Sometimes it may be necessary to roll cast in order to bring your line to the surface. Keep on practicing with different lengths of line until you are proficient, but do not cast beyond fifty feet because the Spey cast exerts a twisting strain on the rod. Of course the old-fashioned sixteen-foot spliced greenheart salmon fly rods were impervious to such stresses!

By adjusting your arc of swing and the dip of the rod tip in the second phase you will be able to place your leader and fly on the water where required, just out of the way of the forward cast. If the fly pitches too far upstream your forward cast will lose power and control.

The Double Spey Cast

Like the single Spey, the double Spey's origin was in salmon fly fishing, and its purpose was to enable the angler to overcome a downstream wind which would blow his line and fly on to him before he could complete the forward cast. However, for the trout fly fisher who is right-handed rather than truly ambidextrous the single Spey cast is used for changing direction towards the right and the double Spey cast for changing direction towards the left. To explain this in a different way, the single Spey is used to fish a nymph or wet fly in a stream flowing from right to left and the double Spey suits a stream flowing from left to right. Of course the opposite would apply to a left-handed caster.

A double Spey is merely a single Spey cast with an additional movement incorporated between the raise and the swing to the right, so there is nothing to be alarmed about once you have overcome the single Spey. In the first phase, raise your rod to eleven o'clock to free the line from the grip of the water. Carry on into the second

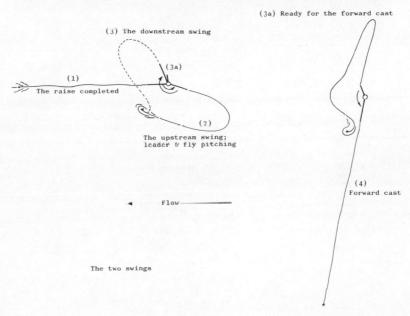

FIGURE 29. Plan of the double Spey cast.

phase by swinging your shoulders, arms and rod to the left (a backhand swing), pitching the fly just to the right of where you want to cast, but without raising the rod to the near-vertical position. In the third phase swing to the right, continuing the motion of your right hand and rod into the position for beginning the forward cast, taking care however not to move the fly from where it pitched; the belly of the line should now form a "D" behind the rod (Figs. 29, 30 and 31). In the fourth phase, make your forward cast as in the single Spey, shooting line and following through. The timing is an even "one-hundred-thousand, two-hundred-thousand, three-hundred-thousand, four-hundred-thousand." As in the single Spey the arcs of your swings will be governed to suit the direction in which you wish to cast.

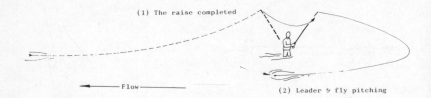

(1) The raise completed

Flow

(2) Leader & fly pitching

FIGURE 30. The upstream swing.

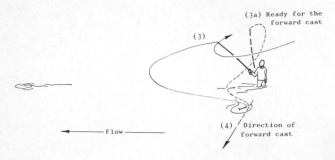

(3a) Ready for the forward cast

(3)

Flow

(4) Direction of forward cast

FIGURE 31. The downstream swing.

After a little practice with the double Spey you will discover how easily the line swings around from upstream to downstream, and, still in motion, sails out lightly in the forward cast. Although the single Spey and double Spey casts are primarily suited to stream fishing, they can be used equally well for fishing still water where a change of direction is desired. On the other hand the single Spey with a reduced arc of swing may also be used to make a new cast in the same direction as the previous one.

6

Derivatives of the Overhead Cast

The Horizontal Cast

In principle a horizontal cast is an overhead cast performed sideways, but since its plane is horizontal instead of almost vertical, the force of gravity affects it in a different way and there are subtle differences in the mechanics of casting. The horizontal cast serves at least two purposes: first to enable the angler to fish under obstructions such as tree branches, and secondly, by keeping the rod low, to avoid spooking a wary fish in clear water.

The horizontal cast is primarily a dry fly cast, so your tackle should include a double-tapered floating line and a general purpose leader with a small fly. Stand with your feet slightly apart and your left foot towards where you are going to cast. The first thing to do is to get the feel of casting in a horizontal plane, so lay about twenty feet of line on the water with the overhead cast, then pick up sideways and make a number of false casts with the rod moving horizontally at your right side. If you imagine a horizontal clock face around you with nine o'clock pointing in the direction of your casts, your rod should be moving back and forth between ten-thirty and twelve-thirty (Fig. 32). Watch your rod carefully to make sure it stays in a horizontal plane all the way, without droop-

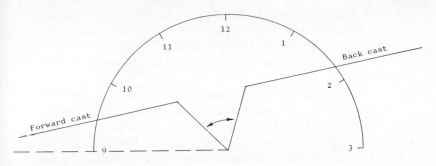

FIGURE 32. Plan of the horizontal cast exercise.

ing at the ends of the arc or lifting. Check that the line is making a narrow entry in front and behind, and that there is sufficient speed in your false casts to keep the line well up. Two or three minutes should suffice for this exercise.

Now you are ready to start on the real horizontal cast. In the first phase, raise your forearm and rod sideways so that they reach a horizontal position at approximately ten o'clock, simultaneously drawing line in with your left hand. Continue into the second phase by speeding up the rod tip in a gradually rising plane to twelve o'clock for the back cast (Fig. 33), drifting the rod to twelve-thirty during the pause. In the third phase, cast forwards

FIGURE 33. False casting.

in a horizontal plane to ten-thirty. In the fourth phase, shoot the line and follow through, lowering your forearm and rod sideways to nine o'clock. Try this a few times until you feel familiar with it, maintaining equal timing for the four phases.

Study Figure 33 for a moment, noting the wedge-shaped orbit of the rod tip in false casting. Pick up the line as before, then make a few false casts while you try to make your rod tip follow this orbit. Don't forget to lower it after each forward false cast, and keep your casting arc restricted between ten-thirty and twelve-thirty (Fig. 32). Finish your cast by shooting your line and following through to nine o'clock.

Pick up the line again and limit yourself to two false casts and a complete cast, shooting to lengthen your line at each of the false casts. Practice with increasing lengths of line, gradually working out to about fifty feet. Try to achieve accuracy by dropping the fly on floating objects in various directions. Keep a wary eye on your rod to ensure that it is still more or less horizontal and following its orbit correctly.

When done properly the horizontal cast has a fair amount of speed, but it is a delicate cast to perform and little effort is necessary. The line should follow a flat trajectory forwards, dropping the fly quickly on the water without any fuss. While the true horizontal cast is carried out in a horizontal plane, there will be occasions when it is desirable to cast in an intermediate plane somewhere between the overhead cast and the horizontal cast.

The Horizontal Lift

Another derivative of the overhead cast, and serving the same two purposes as the horizontal cast, the horizontal lift is adapted to drop a small dry fly extremely lightly.

This cast requires the use of a double-tapered floating

line and a fine tapered leader with a small, light fly. Stand facing to the right of the direction in which you are going to cast, and lay out twenty feet of line.

Pick up the line and continue into the back cast in a gradually rising plane, as for the horizontal cast. During the pause, lower the tip of your rod slightly and make your forward cast in a horizontal plane (Fig. 34), following through with a quarter turn wrist roll to the left to flick the rod tip upwards (Fig. 35) before lower-

FIGURE 34. The horizontal lift.

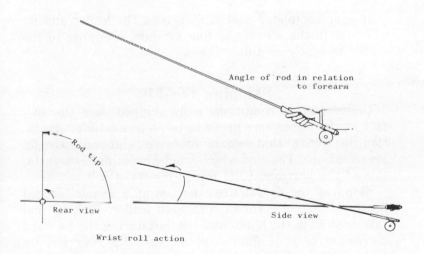

FIGURE 35. The lift.

ing it to within a few inches of the water. The timing is the same as for the overhead cast or a little quicker, and the horizontal arcs are the same as for the horizontal cast (Fig. 32).

Note the orbit followed by the rod tip in false casting (Fig. 34) and compare it with the orbit for the horizontal cast (Fig. 33). Now make some false casts, guiding your rod tip through the horizontal lift orbit, until you are accustomed to the new movements. Then pick up your twenty feet of line and make two false casts, lengthening line by shooting it at each false cast; follow with the complete cast, remembering to roll your wrist in the follow through. The wrist roll is a movement of the wrist similar to turning a key, but it must be done smartly to achieve its effect, and of course the rod must be held at an angle in relation to your forearm (Fig. 35). The height of the lift is controlled by adjusting this angle, a greater angle causing a higher lift, and vice versa.

If your completed cast is a success, the leader and fly will rise in the air as the line extends, dropping to the water as gently as thistledown.

Skipping the Fly

Under certain conditions a fly skipped over the surface of the water may prove to be an irresistible temptation to a fish that would otherwise ignore your fly presentations. The cast which will be explained is a variation of the horizontal lift minus the wrist roll.

Skipping the fly requires the use of a double-tapered floating line and a forward tapered leader. Pick up and false cast as in the horizontal lift, but during the forward movement of your final complete cast dip your rod tip just a little and raise it again, shooting line and following through normally. This action will cause your fly to strike the water on the way to its destination, and the forward tapered leader will then arch forward so that the fly bounces up and over, alighting before the line has had time to fall (Fig. 36).

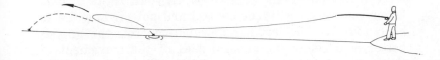

FIGURE 36. Skipping the fly.

The Backhand Cast

The backhand cast is a necessity for those of us who are not entirely ambidextrous. Moreover it has further applications which will be used in performing certain other casts which will be explained later, therefore it should be learned and practiced even by an entirely ambidextrous angler.

Use of the word "entirely" is not made without good reason. Some years ago I had the misfortune to dislocate my right shoulder, and while I was convalescing I decided to go fishing. I can cast a fly reasonably well with my left hand, but every time a fish rose to my fly I reacted by attempting to set the hook with my right hand, which held the line. The task of casting left handed and immediately changing hands was easy enough, but having fished out the cast it was a very clumsy operation to transfer all my loops of line to my right hand without causing a tangle and then to have to transfer the rod to my left hand without interfering with the loops.

Returning to the matter in hand, you will require the double-tapered floating line and a general purpose leader. Take up your casting position facing half left, with your right foot forwards.

The mechanics of the backhand cast are essentially

the same as those of the horizontal cast (refer to Figures 32 and 33) except that the cast is performed backhanded, but the secret of success is to keep the right arm up high so that with the forearm horizontal your right hand is level with your chin (Fig. 37). If your right arm is lower your casts will lack control and power. It will also be found that the left hand, which controls the line, is better held below the general area of the movement of the butt end of the rod instead of behind your left hip.

FIGURE 37. The backhand cast.

Besides enabling you to cast in otherwise difficult locations, the backhand cast is useful when a wind is blowing from your right-hand side too strongly to allow an overhead cast over your right shoulder to be performed with safety. On such occasions a backhand cast which is higher than the horizontal plane will be more convenient, and will be referred to as a backhand-overhead cast.

7

Casting into a Wind

Often I have heard it said that the weather was too rough for fishing—a matter for little concern if the fishing is at one's doorstep, but most frustrating if one happens to be on a fishing trip and time is limited. Yet I have many times fished my fly through a squall and watched others battling successfully against the elements. If one knows how to cast in a high wind, it is merely a question of whether one wishes to fish or not that should influence the decision.

Your line must be a double-tapered line (use the floater for learning), as a forward-tapered line is too dangerous in a strong wind; and your leader must be one of the quick-tapered leaders described in the section devoted to "balanced" tackle. Your fly should be one that offers minimum wind resistance. If the wind is from the left or from straight ahead it will be safe to cast over your right shoulder, but if the wind is from the right a backhand-overhead style of casting will be necessary. Of course, if the wind is behind you everything is in favor of the roll and Spey casts.

The principle of casting in a strong wind is to drop the line on the water before the wind has a chance to blow it around. This can be accomplished by two distinct methods.

The *first* method may be used with either the overhead cast or the backhand-overhead cast. With your right foot forward, make your pick up in the normal way, but throw your back cast higher in the air than usual by transferring the arc slightly forward, say between ten o'clock and twelve o'clock. Aim low near the surface of the water with a fast, powerful forward cast, but make the line form a narrow entry so that it presents minimum wind resistance. Immediately following your forward cast shoot the line and force your elbow up to the right smartly so that the rod tip whips down almost to the water, slamming a downward undulation along the line (Fig. 38). Avoid any tendency to finish the cast in a stooping position.

FIGURE 38.   Finishing the wind cast (first method).

Although the *second* method can only be used in conjunction with the overhead cast over the right shoulder, it is a stronger, more effective cast than the first method, provided that the rod has plenty of backbone. Indeed, its ability to thrust through gale force winds is astonishing.

I recall an occasion when I was fishing from the shore of a small lake with a party of friends, and it was too rough to launch a boat. Spray blew in our faces, and the whitecaps left long streaks of foam behind them. We staggered along the beach with difficulty and began to fish. All of us were having trouble reaching out with our flies to where the fish should have been; casts of fifty or sixty feet were straightening out satisfactorily, but that was not far enough. After half an hour we decided to quit, and as we headed homewards pieces of tree branches hurtled through the air. Later we heard on the radio that winds of one hundred miles per hour had struck the area, so we had been casting fifty or sixty feet of straight line against a one-hundred m.p.h. hurricane!

Today there is merely a brisk breeze blowing off the water, but it will suffice. Learning this wind cast is going to be tiring for your wrist, so stop and have a rest when you need it and don't go on too long.

Hold the rod with your thumb along the top of the grip (refer to Chapter 2, Fig. 6), and stand with your right foot forward. Lay out about forty feet of line. Pick up and throw your back cast high, bringing your right hand close up to your shoulder and swinging your shoulder back. The forward cast is combined with the follow through into one very swift movement: swing your right shoulder forward and thrust your arm and rod out straight, pointing the rod at the spot where you intend to place your fly; then shoot the line from your left hand. This forward movement should be delivered with all the weight of your shoulder swing behind it, like a hard punch, and simultaneously your wrist must force the rod down so that it is in line with your right arm (Fig. 39). The action is similar to a fencing thrust, and when properly carried out has the effect of throwing

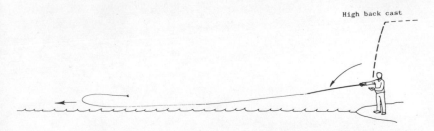

FIGURE 39. The wind cast (second method).

the line extremely fast and low over the water. In summary, the rod movements are: raise, high back cast, and thrust. If your line fails to make a narrow entry or travels forward too high, it is probably because your back casts are not high enough.

Pick up and cast again, shooting more line when you feel you can handle it, until you are casting up to sixty feet or more; make your forward thrusts as fast and decisive as possible. Rest at intervals when your wrist feels sore.

At the end of an hour's wind casting you will probably feel you have had enough. However, after one or two practice sessions you should be sufficiently skilled to defy anything less than a 70 m.p.h. gale.

8

Variations of the Overhead and Backhand Casts

Although these three casts have authentic names, they are actually no more than variations of the overhead and backhand casts or combinations. Presumably they were named for convenience, and since this facilitates their differentiation we shall adhere to their names. For all of these casts a double-tapered floating line and a general purpose tapered leader should be used.

The Galway Cast

The Galway cast is an effective method of casting a wet fly when only a small opening exists for the extension of the line in the back cast. It is particularly useful for fishing streams with overgrown banks or when there are power lines behind. Power lines and cables seem to have a magnetic attraction for trout flies.

Stand facing to the left with your right foot nearest to where you are going to cast, and make a preliminary cast. Now swing to the left without moving your feet or interfering with the rod and line, so that you are looking at the opening where your back cast will be placed. Pick up and aim at this opening with an overhead forward cast over your right shoulder, wait until the line has

extended, and use a backhand cast, or a backhand-
overhead cast over your left shoulder, to drop your fly on
the water.

Next, try the same cast the other way round. Stand
with your left foot toward where your fly is to alight
and face right. Swing on your feet so that you are looking at the opening for your back cast. Pick up and backhand cast into the opening, then swing to the left and
overhead cast on to the water.

The Willows Cast

Serving the same purpose as the Galway cast, the
willows cast is more convenient when false casts are involved, such as in dry fly fishing.

Stand with your left foot nearest to the place where
you wish to drop your fly, make a preliminary cast, and
pivot to the right until you are facing the opening where
your line is to extend. Pick up and false cast with the
overhead cast into the opening, then pivot to the left
and make a final overhead forward cast on to the water
(Fig. 40).

Where conditions warrant the use of the horizontal
cast, it may be used instead of the overhead cast.

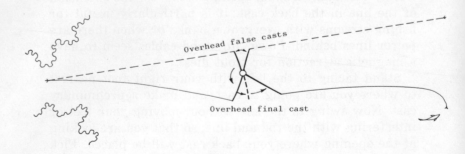

FIGURE 40. Plan of the willows cast.

The Angle Cast

The angle cast is valuable as a change-direction cast, but is also commonly used to place a fly across a stream when the bank is too heavily bushed to allow a normal overhead cast. It permits false casting, therefore it is well suited to dry fly fishing.

Ideally it should be performed with a combination of the overhead cast and the backhand cast (Fig. 41), but if there is insufficient space it can be performed by using only one of these casts without sacrificing too much control (Fig. 42).

If space allows the use of a combination of casts, and it is desired to change direction towards the left, stand with the right foot in the direction from which the fly must be picked up. Pick up and false cast with the overhead cast. After the final back cast, move your arm and rod in front of your face into the backhand position and drop your fly on the water with the backhand cast.

To change direction towards the right by the same method, place your left foot towards the fly. Pick up and cast back with the backhand cast, then swing your arm and rod into the overhead position, making your false

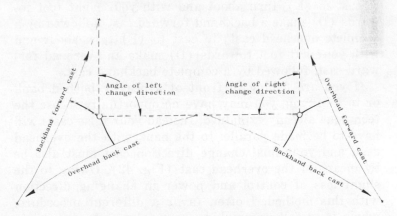

FIGURE 41. Using a combination of casts for changing direction.

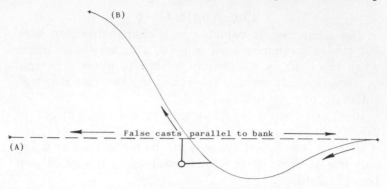

FIGURE 42.   Plan of the angle cast.

casts and final cast over your right shoulder.

Carrying this a step further, refer to Figure 43: to pick up a fly at (A) and cast to anywhere in (B), with your left foot towards (A) use a backhand back cast and an overhead forward cast; to cast it to (C), with your right foot towards (A) use an overhead back cast and a backhand forward cast; to cast to (D) turn about and make an overhead or backhand forward cast from (A); to cast to (E), turn about and with your right foot towards (D) make a backhand forward cast, followed by a complete overhead cast; to cast to (F) turn about and with your left foot towards (D) make an overhead forward cast, followed by a complete backhand cast.

If you are fishing in front of a heavily bushed bank or in a canyon, you may have no opportunity to use the technique already explained. Instead your false casts will have to be made parallel to the bank with the overhead cast, and your final change direction cast must also be by means of the overhead cast (Fig. 42). Owing to the slight loss of control and power in changing direction with this method, I often favor a different procedure, which is as follows: making your false casts parallel to the bank with the overhead cast as before, allow the fly to settle very briefly on the water at (A) (Fig. 42) ; from there pick up and Spey cast to (B). (This manipulation works very well and, in my experience, the dry fly's floating propensity is not at all impaired.)

The practical applications of the angle cast may thus be summarized. First, it is a quick, simple method of changing direction. With it a fly can be picked up and immediately placed in any direction in two or at most three rod movements, saving valuable time if you are presenting the fly to a cruising fish, and eliminating the movements that would otherwise be necessary in achieving the same change of direction by means of a series of false casts. Secondly, it enables a dry fly to be fished across a heavily bushed stream by false casting parallel to the bank and making a final forward cast in a different direction altogether (Fig. 42).

Although neither the Galway Cast, the willows cast, nor the angle cast involves new casting mechanics, the techniques essential to all of them are worthy of careful study and application.

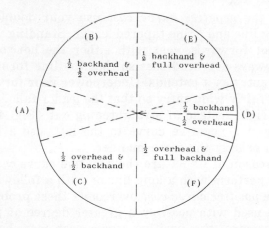

FIGURE 43.   Covering the full circle .

9

Presentational Casting

The Curved Casts

It is desirable to present a floating fly or a nymph to a shy fish in such a manner that the fly enters his sphere of vision before the line and leader, thus commanding his attention and triggering his feeding instincts before he has time to be distracted or become suspicious. To accomplish this it may be necessary to drop the leader on the water so that it curves around like a shepherd's crook.

For the *negative curve cast* use your double-tapered floating line and a fine tapered leader. Standing with your left foot forwards, cast with either the horizontal cast or sideways-overhead cast so that the line forms a horizontal entry as it extends. Underpower your forward cast with a fairly wide entry so that the leader falls in a curve to the right instead of straightening out (Fig. 44).

To cast a negative curve to the left, use a backhand cast in exactly the same manner.

By reason of its nature the negative curve cast is difficult to perform with a long line or with a following wind, but the *positive curve cast* overcomes these problems, and can be used with possibly a greater degree of precision. Furthermore, the positive curve cast may be used to place the fly behind an obstruction such as a rock or floating log.

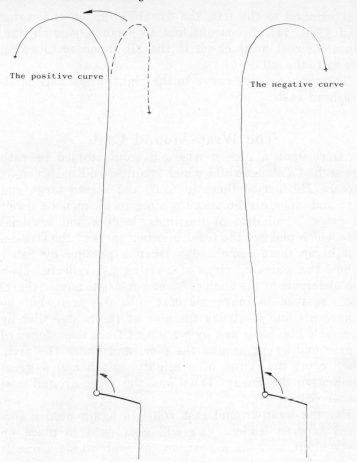

The positive curve

The negative curve

FIGURE 44. Plan of the curved casts.

Tackle for the positive curve should include a double-tapered floating line and a forward tapered leader. To throw a curve to the left, make a sideways-overhead cast with a narrow, almost horizontal entry, and use a little more power than would be necessary to cause the line to extend straight. The forward tapered leader should "cow-tail" around to the left, the fly alighting on the water first (Fig. 44). Be careful not to shoot too much line, since the cast must check in the air in order to swing the fly to the left.

To cast a positive curve to the right, use a backhand-overhead cast.

The Wrap-Around Cast

"Once upon a time a wise old trout resided beneath the arch of a stone bridge which spanned an English chalk stream. He tarried there to feed, and waxed large and fat; and since his lie was invisible to all men he dwelt in peace, unmindful of the lines, leaders and artificial flies which plagued the trout in other parts of the stream. But haply there came a day when a passing fly fisher beheld the widening rings of a rising fish reflected upon the underside of the ancient stonework. The angler thereupon essayed to make his cast into the arch, but by chance his line so struck the pier of the bridge that by a miracle his leader and fly were bent from their forward course and swept around the pier, and under the arch. Then came the sound of a mighty splash and a great commotion did ensue. Thus was the wrap-around cast conceived!"

For the wrap-around cast you will again need a forward tapered leader. You will also need to place an obstruction, such as a post, in the water unless one is already there for your convenience.

Casting with a sideways-overhead cast, calculate your distance from the obstruction so that the last foot or two of line next to the leader will reach it. Then aim a sideways entry at the obstruction, which will cause the leader to "cow-tail" to the left (Fig. 45). To perform a wrap-around cast to the right is more difficult, though it can be done successfully with a backhand cast if everything is in your favor.

FIGURE 45. Plan of the wrap-around cast.

The Bump Cast

The bump cast is used primarily to throw a bass bug on to the water with sufficient zest to advertise its arrival. This conspicuous presentation is also occasionally successful in stimulating a trout into rising, particularly if the fly represents a terrestial insect such as might fall from a tree.

Using a double-tapered floating line with a forward tapered leader, make a fairly high overhead cast, checking the line before it extends fully so that the leader knuckles over, slamming the fly to the surface (Fig. 46). The bump cast is simply an upright version of the positive curve cast. With a little practice you can bump the fly down and cause it to skip or bounce a couple of times towards you on the surface before the line falls by raising the rod slightly as the bump takes place.

The rise of a fish to a bumped fly is usually sudden and furious, so be prepared!

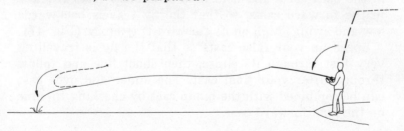

FIGURE 46. The bump cast.

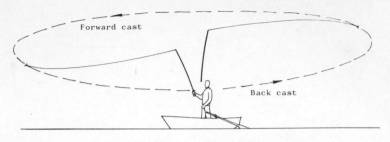

FIGURE 47. The under and over cast.

The Under and Over Cast

Casting a big fly, such as a bass bug, with a trout rod requires a technique of its own. However, it is easily accomplished by making the fly follow an eliptical circuit.

Owing to the bass bug's large size, the leader will need to be stout even at the tip, and here we find an exception to the rule of tapered leaders. A level leader comprising six or eight feet of 15 or 20 pound test nylon will do very nicely with a double-tapered floating line. Making false casts in the overhead style, tilt your rod to the right in the back casts and hold it in an almost vertical plane in the forward casts, so that the fly travels backwards low and swings high on its forward trajectory (Fig. 47).

Speed up your false casts so that the fly is travelling very fast through its elipse, then shoot line and follow through after your final cast. The under and over cast can be combined with the bump cast by checking the line on the final forward cast.

10

Restricted Casting

All the casts in this chapter are used for fishing under difficulties from closely confined positions. Therefore they do not in themselves provide the satisfaction and pleasure associated with the casts previously explained, rather they are a means to an end, and it is well that they should be included in the fly fisher's repertoire. For all of them a double-tapered floating line and general purpose tapered leader should be used.

The Short Cast

Very occasionally it is necessary to approach to within a few feet of a fish in order to place your fly where it can be seen. Usually such an approach has to be made slowly and with extreme caution to avoid disturbing the fish, and the fly must be presented from a crouching, or even a prone position, on the bank. After so much trouble, there must be no error in the presentation of the fly.

Let us imagine that the bank offers some form of cover, such as long grass. Taking plenty of time, and making your movements as quietly as though you were robbing a light sleeper, pull out as much line as you will need from the rod tip. Then try to assume such a position that the rod tip will just reach the edge of the bank. Grasping the rod grip in your right hand, place your left thumb over the butt and your left palm and fingers against the reel. Your left hand will help steady the rod. Now, keeping the rod as low as possible, wave it gently once backwards and once forwards, praying that the fly will alight perfectly! The steadying action of the left hand is the key to casting only a few feet; without it, you will be surprised to discover how difficult it is to achieve absolute control and precision.

The Tower Cast

I have heard it said that the tower, or steeple, cast is as much a myth as the Indian rope trick, which nobody admits to have witnessed. Whether you will ever have an opportunity to witness the Indian rope trick or not remains to be seen, but there is probably no valid reason why you cannot perform the tower cast yourself.

The principle of the tower cast is to throw the line vertically upward above the rod, whence a forward movement of the rod extends it over the water.

Stand with your right foot forwards. Keeping your right hand as low down as possible and close to your right hip, in the first phase raise the rod to forty-five degrees to assemble the belly of the line under the rod tip. While the line is still moving, lift your right hand and rod as high up as you can reach in one swift movement in the second phase, keeping your rod at forty-five degrees all the way. This will cause your line to extend upwards in a big question mark (Fig. 48); while it is travelling upwards, move the rod into a vertical position and bend your right elbow, bringing your hand down to your shoulder. In the third phase, to counteract the downward trend of the line, aim a high overhead forward cast, extending your arm and rod in a thrusting movement. Shoot as much line as possible, and follow through low in the

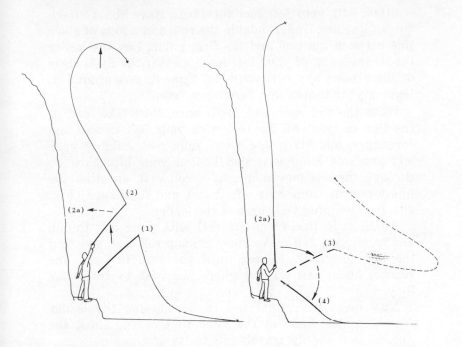

FIGURE 48. The tower cast.

fourth phase. The timing is approximately equal for the four phases.

The tower cast is good for only relatively short casts up to forty or fifty feet with a trout rod. It is easiest to perform from a high bank.

The Snap Roll Cast

Sometimes a situation arises when the roll cast is the one and only cast that would serve to place the fly, but if the fly should be a dry fly the roll cast would not be suitable on account of its tendency to drown a floating fly. Such a situation calls for the snap roll.

Stand with your left foot forwards. Have about fifteen feet of line and leader outside the rod, and a loop of slack line between the reel and the first guide. Lay the leader across the palm of your left hand so that the fly is clear of the ground and curl your last three fingers around it, leaving your thumb and forefinger free.

Wave the rod back and forth once, then take hold of the line in front of the reel with your left thumb and forefinger, and strip line from your reel, holding your left arm and hand extended behind your hip. Now go through the rod movements of a roll cast, shooting the line forwards from your left thumb and forefinger (Fig. 49), but retaining your grip of the leader.

Again strip line from the reel with your left thumb and forefinger, and make another snap roll cast, shooting the line forwards. Repeat until the loop in your line reaches about half-way to where you wish to drop your fly.

Now make your final roll cast, releasing the leader from your left hand at the same time as you shoot the line, so that the fly travels out to its destination.

Since the fly has been kept dry throughout the entire procedure, it will float as well as though it had been put on the water with an overhead cast. However, since no

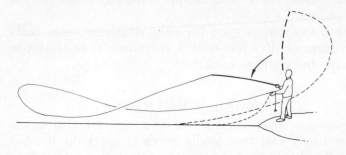

FIGURE 49. The snap roll cast.

false casting is possible from such a position, the leader
and fly should be dried with a handkerchief between casts
and the fly oiled as often as required.

The Bowspring Cast

The circumstances which make the bowspring cast
necessary constitute a fly fisher's nightmare! Imagine a
tangled mass of growth along a bank with deep water
below, and big fish cruising by as they feed on insects
that have dropped from the overhanging branches; the
only opening will just permit a rod to be poked through it.
Such is the environment for this cast.

Have as much line as you will need outside the rod to
place your fly (probably fifteen feet is about the maximum). Hold the leader and the fly in your left hand and
poke the rod through the hole between the bushes. Pull
the leader and fly back with the left hand so that the rod
is bent upwards like a bow (Fig. 50), and taking careful
aim, let go the leader and fly.

Fortunately for the author it is not within the scope
of this book to suggest what has to be done in such circumstances after a fish has been hooked.

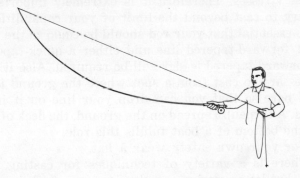

FIGURE 50. The bowspring cast.

11

Casting a Long Line

Tournament casting has done for fishing what warfare has done for aviation. All kinds of new techniques have been developed and equipment has undergone vast improvements. Although we are not going to attempt tournament casting in these pages, we shall however be utilizing some of the same techniques for casting a long line.

The stresses inflicted upon a fly rod in casting more than eighty feet are very severe, and any faults in timing or technique will be greatly amplified, thus increasing those stresses. Therefore it is extremely important not to try to cast beyond the limit of your capabilities, and it is essential that your rod should be equal to the task.

A forward-tapered line and either a quick-tapered or a forward-tapered leader will be required. Also it will be necessary to cast from a spot where the ground is clean and bare so that you can drop your line on it in loose coils. A tarpaulin spread on the ground, the deck of a raft, or the bottom of a boat fulfills this role.

For your own safety wear a hat.

There is a variety of techniques for casting a long line, but let us confine ourselves to one, which is perhaps the simplest.

Stand with your right foot forwards, and hold the rod

with your thumb along the top of the grip. Lengthen line
by false casting with the overhead cast until the "hinge"
is reached. This can be found by casting slightly more line
than will pick up and cast cleanly, and shortening it until
its optimum length is ascertained (it is a good idea to
paint a few inches of line at the hinge so that it will be
clearly visible; indeed some forward-tapered lines are
manufactured which incorporate a distinguishing mark).
The "hinge" is likely to be a little over fifty feet from
the line's forward tip.

Next, strip about twenty feet of line from your reel,
letting it drop on the ground in front. Rearrange it in
loose coils on the ground at your left side, so that the coils
are in their correct order for shooting, the top coil being
the first to pass through the guides. Holding the line in
your left hand, use the roll pick-up and overhead cast
to lay down your line again, shooting all the coils from the
ground. The length of this cast will amount to roughly
seventy-five feet.

Strip another twenty feet of line from the reel and
rearrange the coils as before. Now draw in line through
the rod guides until you come to the "hinge," placing the
retrieved line carefully on top of the coils on the ground.

Again use the roll pick-up, but make your back cast
sideways in a steeply rising plane; and while the line is
extending behind, raise your left hand with the line so
that it closely approaches your right, in the meantime
allowing the rod to drift back to two o'clock (Fig. 51).

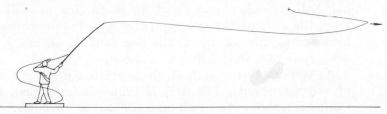

FIGURE 51. The back cast extending.

During your back cast, swing your body to the right and rock back slightly on your feet. Watch the line extending behind you.

As soon as the line has extended, swing your body to the left and rock forwards on your feet; at the same time strip line in through the guides by a vigorous downward and backward movement of your left arm and hand, force the rod forwards in a vertical plane and exert pressure on the grip with your right thumb in a swift, decisive hammer-blow action (Fig. 52). Check the rod at ten

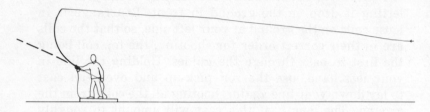

FIGURE 52. Making the forward cast.

o'clock, and when your line has about half extended in the air in front of you move your left hand forward close to the first guide *without* shooting. When the line has reached its full extent in the air, make another false cast in exactly the same manner but speed up the line's rate of travel by stripping in line faster with your left hand and putting all the drive you can into the rod movements. In the third cast you should develop your maximum speed; check the rod at ten o'clock, wait until the line has half extended, and shoot as much line as will go from the coils on the ground (Fig. 53). Follow through by lowering the rod tip as the line falls. If all has gone well, your cast should finish as shown in figure 54.

As you must have noticed, there are two distinct kinds of rod movements. The first is immediate reaction, for example, raising the rod, and following through; the

FIGURE 53. Shooting line.

second is stored reaction. The function of the rod in storing reaction may be likened to that of a spring. Hence its power to straighten has a direct bearing on the speed, and consequently the momentum, imparted to the line. This is therefore a limiting factor affecting the length of your casts. The other prime factor is, of course, your own physical strength combined with stability; much practice will increase your casting strength, but stability

FIGURE 54. A perfect finish.

is somewhat dependent on weight. For trout fishing purposes, however, casts in excess of ninety or one-hundred feet are wholly unwarranted and punish the rod severely.

At first your casts will have to be made slowly and carefully, particular attention being given to timing and technique rather than results. It takes several weeks of practice to work up a consistent distance of more than ninety feet, which is a very good standard to achieve, although I have met a few enthusiasts who claim to have cast up to one hundred and twenty feet with ordinary fishing gear.

Salmon Fly Casting

Casting with the double-handed salmon fly rod is a unique experience. There is a thrill in the bold sweep of the long, powerful rod, in the easy lift of the long line to the surface, in its clean pick up and graceful back cast, and in the forward cast, reaching far out across the water, effortless and unhurried yet massive in its thrust. It is synonymous with fishing wide, fast rivers for big fish.

Although it is often regarded as obsolete, there are four reasons why a salmon fly rod is supreme for its tasks. First, the large, heavy flies generally used in this type of fishing, almost unmanageable with a trout rod, are handled easily with a salmon rod. Secondly, long casts are the order of the day, and the salmon rod performs them beautifully. Thirdly, the long reach of a salmon fly rod provides for easy control of a long line in the water. And fourthly, the power in a salmon rod is capable of bringing heavy fish to gaff (or beach) through strong currents without the rod suffering undue strain.

The popularity of salmon fly fishing has been generally confined to the countries of north-western Europe, where it was originated and has been developed to its present status. In those countries, where riparian ownership prevails, salmon fly fishing of any quality is so much sought after that its value is beyond the reach of all but the most wealthy sportsmen.

However, many rivers of the North American continent are just made for salmon fly fishing with both sunk fly and greased line. Such rivers as contain runs of Atlantic salmon, very big rainbow trout and steelhead are admirably suited to salmon fly fishing. For example, in some of the larger streams of British Columbia, with which I am familiar, salmon fly fishing, although practiced by a very small minority of anglers in comparison to the number of bait fishers, can be extremely effective.

Yet so little appears to be known about the art of salmon fly fishing with the double-handed rod on the American continent that perhaps a brief explanation of its principles may assist towards a better comprehension of the casts associated with it. The methods of fishing for steelhead and very big rainbow trout in rivers with the double-handed fly rod being much the same as those of fishing for Atlantic salmon, I use the general term "salmon fly fishing."

There are two entirely different techniques involved in salmon fly fishing, namely sunk fly and greased line. The sunk fly is fished close to the bottom with a line that is designed to sink. Generally, particularly when the water temperature is low or when the water is colored by a runoff from melting snow or heavy rains, sunk flies are used in the larger sizes of 1/0 to 3/0. They must fish close to the bottom, for mid-water fishing is almost always useless. The sunk fly is usually cast at about forty-five degrees across and downstream, and allowed to fish around in the currents until it is more or less below the angler, much as a spinning lure is fished. For the best effect the sunk fly needs to be at the end of a long line, fished slowly.

The right time to fish the greased line is when the water is fining down after the spring runoff, particularly in conditions of bright sunshine, warm air, and little or no wind; and sometimes in the fall too, when the same conditions apply. In the height of summer when the rivers are low, salmon fly tackle should give way to trout tackle. The size of the fly should depend upon the water temperature, small flies being used when temperatures are relatively warm, and larger flies when the water is colder.

Flies for greased line fishing are lightly dressed and slender in appearance, and are fished just below the surface. Therefore all but the last few feet of fly line must float. In greased line fishing the fly should be presented to the fish broadside or in such a manner that it "swims" across the currents without "drag." This is accomplished by "mending" the line as often as it becomes necessary. When a fish rises to a greased line fly no immediate attempt should be made to set the hook, as often the take is very slow.

Since greased line flies are dressed on very thin, sharp hooks, there is even a tendency for fish to hook themselves if left to their own devices. Rather the idea is to "lead" the fly with the rod as it fishes around, and the angler should tighten his line by swinging the rod downstream and towards his own bank assisted by the action of the currents in cushioning against the line. In this way fish taken on the greased line are usually hooked very firmly in the corner of the mouth. It requires a great deal of self-discipline to see a big fish rise to the surface and take the fly, and to refrain from the natural impulse of "striking," but that is one of the tantalizing attractions of greased line fishing, and moreover, if a fish misses the fly on its first attempt to take, it is likely to swim around and intercept the fly again. Hence it pays to continue fishing as though nothing had happened until the line stops or a pull is felt.

Thus the techniques of sunk fly and greased line

salmon fishing are complementary to one another, each particularly well suited to its special circumstances, and each proven to be effective on the rivers of the New World. I hope that the chapters which follow will enable more Canadians and Americans to acquire the skills of fly fishing with the long rod and to enjoy to a greater extent the fruits of their heritage.

12

"Balanced" Salmon Fly Tackle

As in the first part of this book, we are concerned with only the items of equipment for casting, namely rods, reels, lines and leaders. Ideally the salmon fly fisher should be equipped with at least two outfits; one for "heavy duty" fishing with big sunk flies in strong water, and the other for greased line fishing with small flies in lower water conditions. It would be difficult to effect a compromise except for smaller streams.

It would appear that at the present time practically all salmon fly fishing tackle is made in Great Britain, and since this type of equipment is so specialized I feel bound to quote the various items from catalogues at my disposal together with their manufacturers' names. However, owing to the rapid upward trend in prices today, any reference to cost would soon be redundant. If I offend by omitting the names of companies manufacturing tackle similar to any I have listed, this is to be regretted, and I wish to emphasize that such omissions are not intended.

There are several very excellent greased line salmon fly rods on the market, among them Hardy Brothers' (Alnwick, England) "L.R.H. Greased Line Rod," 13 ft., approx. 18 oz.; Hardy's "Wye Salmon Fly Rod" in the 12½ ft. length, approx. 18 oz., Sharpe's (Aberdeen, Scotland) "Impregnated Swelled Spliced Rod" in the 13 ft.

length, approx. 16¼ oz., Milward's (Redditch, England) "Flyranger" in the 12½ ft. length, approx. 18½ oz., and Milward's "Flyversa SFR" 12 ft., 10 ins., approx. 21 oz.

At the time of writing Milward's "Flyversa" is a new development which I have not seen, but its principle of construction seems remarkably sound. The cane under the handle becomes thinner towards the butt cap, allowing greater butt flexibility for "mending" line, and, it is claimed, for exceptional casting performance with both heavy salmon fly lines and light trout fly lines.

Spliced built cane salmon rods are not so new. I had occasion to see one of Farlow's "Denham Series" spliced salmon fly rods in the hands of Major L. R. Dunne at an international casting tournament in England in 1937 as well as during many hard practice sessions which preceded the tournament. It was a beautiful rod to handle and a great success. When I tried the rod myself the experience gave me much pleasure. Although unfortunately I believe these rods are no longer made by Farlow's, Sharpe's "Impregnated" rods have a very good reputation indeed. The advantages of spliced rods as opposed to ferrule-jointed rods are two-fold: first, the splices do not interfere with the action of the rod, insomuch as the rod behaves as one continuous length of cane; and secondly, a spliced rod will stand up to the torsion exerted by prolonged Spey casting whereas an ordinary ferrule-jointed rod will not. It stands to reason that casting should always be carried out with the splices square on to the direction of rod movement; this habit is easily acquired.

Since most of your casts with the sunk fly outfit are likely to be Spey casts, the stresses imposed on a salmon rod by prolonged Spey casting should be taken into consideration. The rod for this type of work should be 13½ ft. to 14 ft. in length. There are two outstanding rods which should answer the purpose particularly well; one is Sharpe's "Impregnated Swelled Spliced Rod" in the 14 ft. length, approx. 18¾ oz., and the other is Hardy's "L.R.H. Spey Casting Rod," 13 ft., 9 ins., approx. 22½ oz. (this is a ferruled rod that has been specially designed and tested to withstand Spey casting).

In checking over a new salmon fly rod, first make sure that you like the "feel" of its action by waving the rod to and fro. Its curve should be evenly distributed, without hint of weakness in any section. Holding the rod horizontal, sight along its top to see that it is straight while you turn it over slowly. Examine the fittings and inspect the entire rod for blemishes. If several rods are available, compare them before making your final choice.

Turning to reels, you will need a 3¾ ins. or 4 ins. diameter salmon fly reel with a wide drum for your greased line outfit, to which should be firmly attached 300 ft. or more of 25 lb. test backing line; and a 4 ins. salmon fly reel for your sunk fly outfit, to which is attached 300 ft. or more of 30 lb. test backing. I favor the type of reel with a revolving back plate; in my experience its construction is far less subject to friction and the wear and tear of fighting big fish than the ordinary type with a simple drum which revolves on a spindle attached to the frame; also it enables one to exert finger pressure against the plate to act as a sensitive brake in an emergency. For rods of more than 14 ft. in length (one still sees the occasional fifteen footer), a 4½ ins. reel holding up to 450 feet of 35 lb. test backing as well as fly line would be suitable. A non-rusting metal line-guard will save unnecessary line wear. The weight of the reel is of little importance in salmon fly fishing.

Some of the rods mentioned earlier have screw-grip reel fittings, therefore they should be matched with reels with the corresponding type of seat. Hardy's "L.R.H. Greased Line Rod," "Wye" rod, and "L.R.H. Spey Casting Rod" all fall within this category. For all of them

Hardy's "Perfect" salmon fly reel is admirably suited.
Indeed the "Perfect" is one of the very few reels now
available with a revolving back plate, besides being
beautifully made; therefore it would be the reel of my
choice for all salmon fly rods. Although its seat is grooved
to take the screw-grip fittings of Hardy's rods, this should
not interfere with its use on rods having fittings of another type.

Salmon fly lines which are to be used solely for greased
line fishing should of course float. On the other hand
there are sure to be occasions when you will wish to fish
a sunk fly with your greased line outfit, and I therefore
suggest the use of Terylene Polyester fly lines for both
your greased line and sunk fly outfits. For greased line
fishing you can rub in as required a suitable floatant dressing (Milward's "Floatmaster" or "Flotit," or standard
"Mucilin"; but *not* a silicone dressing for Terylene or
nylon lines). The floatant dressing can be removed with
detergent when you want the line to sink. Both your outfits must include double-tapered lines, although very occasionally a forward-tapered salmon fly line might be used
to advantage. Salmon fly lines are usually manufactured
from waterproof silk or Terylene Polyester yarn, and of
the two I prefer Terylene, first, because it is rot-proof
and trouble-free, and secondly, owing to its higher spe-
cific gravity it sinks more readily when not greased.
Hardy's "Corolene" and Milward's "Flycraft" fly lines
are both made from Terylene. Milward's "Twincraft"
line, of nylon for one half of its length, giving excellent
floatability when greased, and Terylene for its other half,
seems to offer interesting possibilities as an alternative
choice for your greased line outfit. Each half is only
sixty feet long, but with the length of your rod and leader
added amounts to over eighty feet, which would give you
sufficient distance for most greased line fishing requirements. Double-tapered salmon fly lines are made in forty
yard lengths.

Name of Rod	Length	Approx. Weight	Reel Diam.	Backing Test Strength	Hardy's "Corolene" Fly Line*	Milward's Flycraft Line
Greased Line Rods						Twincraft or FCF
Hardy's "L.R.H. Greased Line"	13 ft.	18 oz.	4 ins.	25 lb.	FCF	EBg or FCF
Hardy's "Wye"	12½ ft.	18 oz.	3¾ ins.	25 lb.	FCF	EBg or FCF
Milward's "Flyranger"	12½ ft.	18½ oz.	3¾ ins.	25 lb.	FCF	EBg
Milward's "Flyversa SFR"	12'10"	21 oz.	4 ins.	25 lb.	FCF	EBg or FCF
Sharpe's " Impregnated Spliced"	13 ft.	16¼ oz.	4 ins.	25 lb.	FCF	EBg or FCF
Sunk Fly Rods						
Hardy's "L.R.H. Spey Casting"	13'9"	22½ oz.	4 ins.	30 lb.	DAD	EBg or DAD
Sharpe's "Impregnated Spliced"	14 ft.	18¾ oz.**	4 ins.	30 lb.	DAD	EBg or DAD

* The only "Corolene" double-tapered salmon fly lines listed in a recent Hardy's Catalogue are F.C.F. and D.A.D.

** 18¾ oz. seems to be on the light side for a 14 ft. rod, but spliced rods are lighter than ferruled rods of the same power.

The letters denote line thicknesses, their dimensions being approximately as follows:

A.	B.	C.	D.	E.	F.	G (or g)
.060 in.	.055 in.	.050 in.	.045 in.	.040 in.	.035 in.	.030 in.

Correct balance of the line to the rod is of paramount importance. The preceding table shows which double-tapered line would balance each of the rods listed. Milward's double-tapered EBg "Flycraft" line has an extra fine tip added at the "g" end for use with small flies and fine leaders, which is very useful.

Other salmon fly rods, reels and lines are of course available, particularly in the sunk fly range, but I have chosen to list only those which are outstanding for reasons already mentioned.

When you have chosen your line, see that it is firmly spliced on to the backing on your reel, unless it is a Milward's EBg double-tapered "Flycraft" or FCF "Twin-craft" line, in which case a small loop whipped at the end may be attached to a larger loop in the backing; you may wish to turn either of these lines about and fish with the other end quite frequently.

Tapered leaders are not nearly so important for salmon fly casting as they are for trout fly casting. However, I think they help to place the fly neatly. Salmon fly leaders are generally nine feet long, and if you taper your leaders through three thicknesses of equal lengths of limp nylon they should serve your requirements. For very small flies longer leaders in four sections are better. Three sets of tapered leaders, made up from limp nylon, are shown below. (Please refer to the first chapter for instructions on how to make leaders.)

Stout—sunk fly	Medium—small sunk fly or large greased line fly	Fine—greased line
3 ft. 30 lb. test " 20 lb. test " 15 lb. test	3 ft. 20 lb. test " 15 lb. test " 10 lb. test	3 ft. 20 lb. test " 15 lb. test " 10 lb. test " 6 lb. test
total length 9 ft.	total length 9 ft.	total length 12 ft.

Many salmon fly fishers still prefer to use Spanish silkworm gut instead of nylon for their leaders. The best gut is more reliable than nylon and casts better, but it involves more trouble and is much more expensive. So long as you remember to check your leader now and then while fishing, particularly after it has been strained, nylon should see you through. Certainly for learning the casts which follow and practicing them the use of silkworm gut would be unjustified.

Silkworm gut in the heavier sizes is extremely difficult to procure, but if you want to experience the joys of fishing with a really superb leader I recommend that you make up a tapered "collar" of three slightly tapered gut leaders twisted together by hand and bound with fly tying thread at intervals of a few inches. Make a loop at each end of the "collar," fixing the loops in position in the same way as a rope is spliced, and binding over the ends of the splices with tying thread. The "collar" should be between four and a half feet and six feet long. To the fine end of this "collar" will be attached the loop of a single-strand gut leader. The gut "collar" should last for a very long time and withstand a great deal of hard work, but the single-strand leader will need to be replaced fairly frequently. Gut needs to be soaked to soften it before knotting or use. It may be carried between two damp felt pads in a flat tobacco can, or in a silkworm gut leader damper as sold for this purpose.

There is little or nothing to be gained from the use of salmon flies for the sole purpose of casting, so pieces of wool will be quite adequate. Use small wool tags with your greased line outfit, and larger ones with your sunk fly outfit.

For notes on the care of your tackle, please refer to the conclusion of the first chapter.

13

The Roll Cast

Roll casts are very easily performed with the salmon fly rod, whose action is better suited to this style of casting than the quicker action of the trout rod. One of the two basic casts, the roll cast is extremely useful for freeing the line from the water as a preliminary to one of the other casts.

The pull of strong currents on a long, heavy line is integral to salmon fly fishing. Therefore, if it is at all possible, choose a river for your salmon fly casting. In any event your casting sessions must be carried out on water. The ideal place for learning would be a gravel bar in the middle of a river, with adequate clear space for casting. From the opposite sides of such a bar you could practice casting right-handed and left-handed very conveniently. The next best thing would be to wade in some shallows, which is as close as you can get to true fishing conditions. In all probability, however, the ideal set-up will not be available, nevertheless practice at a river if you can, rather than at the local pond, but not from a high bank.

Your tackle for learning and practicing the roll cast will be your sunk fly outfit, consisting of a rod that will stand up to roll casts and Spey casts, a four-inch reel with a forty-yard double-tapered salmon fly line of the correct weight to balance your rod, and a stout tapered leader with a sizable woollen tag for a fly. The line should be attached to the leader with a figure eight knot (Chapter 2, Fig. 4), and the wool may be secured to the leader with a slip-knot.

All casts with the salmon fly rod should be learned and practiced both right-handed and left-handed. Let us begin by roll casting over the right shoulder, with the water flowing from right to left.

Stand with your left foot downstream, and have about twenty feet of line and leader clear of the rod tip, as well as another five feet of slack line between the reel and the first guide. Hold the rod with your right hand close to the top of the grip and your left hand at the butt (Fig. 55). Your hold should be firm but not tense. The forefinger of your right hand will hold the line against the rod grip. Swing the rod back and forth once, letting the slack line slip from your right hand. Placing the butt against your body, pull out another ten feet of line from the reel with your left hand, and hold it as before with your right hand. Wave your rod over the water, allowing the current to drag the slack line from your right hand through the guides. If you have to practice in still water, wave the rod back and forth until all the line is out in front of you. Now you have about thirty-five feet of line and leader outside your rod.

Holding the line against the rod grip with your right forefinger as before to prevent more line from pulling off the reel, lower the rod tip and allow the current to straighten your line downstream. You are ready to begin roll casting.

In the first phase, raise the rod into a nearly vertical position, at the same time lifting your arms as high as you can reach comfortably. This movement must be a positive upward lift and will serve to bring most of the line to the surface against the current. In the second phase, lower the rod to forty-five degrees or ten-thirty if

FIGURE 55. How to hold a salmon rod.

we imagine the upper half of a vertical clock face. Proceed immediately with the third phase by holding the rod butt in your left hand against the front of your left hip, and swinging your body and rod (still at forty-five degrees) around to the right in a one-hundred and twenty degrees arc (Fig. 56); continue the swing by bringing your right hand in close to your shoulder. In the fourth phase, swing your body to the left and force your right arm out to its full extent in a downstream direction, still holding the rod butt against the front of your left hip, and making this forward cast in an almost vertical plane (Figs. 57 and 58). There is no timing for the first phase, but for the second, third and fourth phases the timing should be even, counting "one-two-three, one-two-three, one-two-three" (slow waltz time) for these last three phases, and blending all the movements as smoothly as possible. During the right swing the line follows the arc of the rod tip (Fig. 56), but the leader and fly should

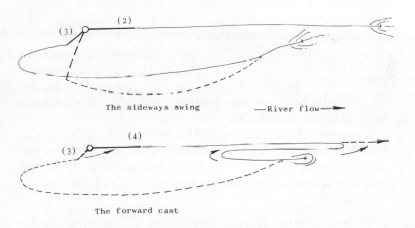

The sideways swing   —River flow—➤

The forward cast

FIGURE 56. Plan of the roll cast.

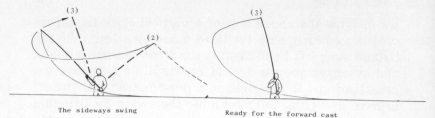

The sideways swing   Ready for the forward cast

FIGURE 57. The third phase.

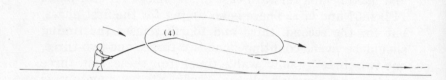

FIGURE 58. The forward cast.

drag over the surface without lifting. As you bring your right hand in towards your shoulder the momentum imparted to the line by the swing will cause it to form a "D" behind the rod (phase 3, Fig. 57). The forward movement of the rod in the final phase throws the "D" forwards so that it pulls the remainder of the line, the leader and the fly with it, and the cast extends straight downstream again (phase 4, Fig. 58).

Practice the roll cast with this short line until you get the feel of the rod and your co-ordination improves to the extent that nearly all your casts are successful. In the meantime, check that you are making none of the following faults:

1. Poor timing. If your phases are too hurried the fly may leave the water during the sideways swing or flick into the air before your rod has finished its forward movement.

2. Lifting the rod back instead of swinging it around in a one-hundred and twenty degrees arc.
3. Failure to make your forward cast with the rod in a vertical plane (the right hand must be brought close in to the shoulder in the third phase).
4. Insufficient drive to your forward cast to carry the line and leader out to their full extent.
5. Checking your rod too high in the forward cast. The right arm must be fully extended.
6. Allowing your left hand, which holds the butt, to move from its correct position against your body during the second, third or fourth phases.
7. Hesitation or jerky movements. The entire cast must be carried out in a smooth rhythm of movement.

When you have overcome all your difficulties, let your line hang in the current while you pull out a few more feet of line from the reel with your left hand. Hold your right fore-finger against the line so that it cannot run out, and make another roll cast, releasing (or "shooting") this additional line before the rod comes to rest after the forward cast.

Instead of raising your rod high and vertically for the first phase of the next cast, raise it to forty-five degrees and draw in a few feet of line through the guides with your left hand, holding it in loose coils between your left thumb and forefinger (Fig. 55). In the British Isles, where salmon rivers and their banks are kept clear of debris, it is usual to allow the slack line to fall where it will; but I have found it quite easy, and far better in less sophisticated waters, to hold the slack in coils with the lower hand to prevent it from becoming snagged. This shortening of the line with the rod at forty-five degrees should bring the line to the surface against the pull of the current. Immediately continue into the second phase by increasing the raise of the rod to about sixty degrees, and the third and fourth phases, releasing the line from your right forefinger and at the same time allowing the coils of slack line to run from your left hand before your rod has quite finished its forward arc.

Continue to practice until you have mastered the art of "shooting" the line and learned to time it perfectly, then lengthen the line by a few more feet, repeating the performance. When you are able to cast sixty feet or more with complete assurance, reel in and move to where the flow of the river is from left to right and start all over again left-handed, with your hands in the opposite positions, making your movements to correspond.

There is no need to thrash your rod down at the water. Rather let your forward cast be a quick driving movement to about ten o'clock and thereafter a deceleration to a smooth stop which is helped by shifting your balance slightly on to your downstream foot.

All your casts have been made downstream. This is because the roll cast does not allow for a change of direction upstream; therefore it is unsatisfactory for fishing a river. Yet the roll cast serves a very useful purpose by freeing your line from the water in preparation for a different cast, and once you have mastered it you should experience little difficulty with the casts that are derived from it.

Keep your practice sessions short; one hour at a time is sufficient. But try to make them as frequent as twice a week so that you will not lose your co-ordination or forget what you have already learned.

14

Overhead Casting

Although the overhead casts require a great deal of space for their back casts, they are of great importance in fishing either a greased line or a sunk fly. Since greased line fishing is properly accomplished only with fine tackle and a relatively light rod, the overhead casts should be used whenever possible with the greased line since they do not impose the severe stresses on a rod that are associated with Spey casting. Moreover, the overhead casts are pleasing to perform and to see performed correctly.

Although flowing water is not an absolute necessity for learning and practicing the overhead casts, it does help enormously in the process of bringing the line to the surface and making a clean pick up. However, plenty of room for the back cast is a vital factor.

I suggest that you alternate between your sunk fly and greased line outfits, starting with the sunk fly outfit for your first session of overhead casting. So your tackle will be the same as for roll casting.

In your second and fourth sessions you will be using your greased line rod and reel with an FCF or EBg double-tapered line (the "g" or fine end next to the leader), and a medium leader with a much smaller woollen tag than before.

The Overhead Swing Cast

Since we shall begin by casting over the right shoulder, the river must be flowing from right to left. Stand with your left foot downstream and place about thirty-five feet of line on the water downstream from you with the roll cast. Hold the line against the grip of your rod with the forefinger of your right hand, so that no more line can be pulled from the reel. For the time being it will be wise to concentrate all your attention on the cast itself, without the added problem of shooting line.

Carry out the first phase of the overhead cast by raising your rod to forty-five degrees (ten-thirty), to bring your line to the surface. In the second phase, holding the butt stationary against the front of your left hip with your left hand, swing your shoulders slightly to the right and simultaneously lift your right hand up smartly so that it is close to and in front of your shoulder. Hold your rod so that it points to about twelve-thirty while the line extends fully behind you (Fig. 59). As soon as it has extended, swing your shoulders slightly to the left and partly extend your right arm, driving the rod forwards to ten-thirty in the third phase (Fig. 60). Check it there without completely stopping it, and follow through in the fourth phase by lowering the tip to within a foot or so of the water, keeping the tip pointing at the line as it extends forward and drops to the surface (Fig. 60).

The movements should be carried out smoothly and in even timing: raise, back cast, forward cast, follow through, or "one-and-*two*-and-*three*-and-four," said slowly. Probably the "entries" or loops formed in the line while it is extending in the back cast and forward cast will be wide at first, and your line may travel back and forth in a low trajectory. If this is the case, put a little more drive into the two power movements of the cast, and at the same time shorten your arcs of power slightly. Concentrate chiefly on your back cast, for your forward

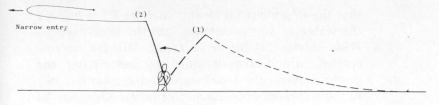

FIGURE 59. The back cast.

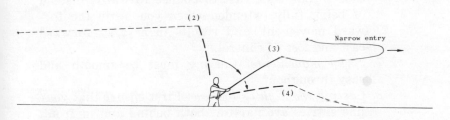

FIGURE 60. The forward cast.

cast cannot be successful after a bad back cast. When your line falls in a heap, use the roll cast to straighten it out, and as soon as it has extended accelerate smoothly into your next overhead back cast. This is *the roll pick-up*.

Practice at this for a while, being careful to avoid the following common faults:

1. *Timing too hurried or uneven.* "Whip cracking" behind denotes a too-hurried forward cast or a weak back cast.

2. *Moving your rod too far back in the second phase.* Hold the butt close to your body with your left hand, and see that it stays there.

3. *Rough pick-up.* If the line does not surface adequately during the raise (first phase), use the roll pick-up. Try to time the first and second phases so

that the line picks up cleanly and the fly is leaving the water as you accelerate into the back cast.

4. *Wide entries behind or in front.* Aim for narrow entries, which are obtained by restricting the power movements (backward and forward casts) to their correct arcs. Excessive power arcs may be caused by allowing the butt of the rod to wander.

5. *Insufficient power to extend the line behind or in front.* Use a little more drive from your shoulder.

6. *Rod creeping forwards during the pause.* This causes your back cast to bounce forwards instead of being fully extended when you begin the forward movement, and results in a jerky forward cast and loss of control.

7. *Jerky movements.* Casting must be smooth and easy throughout.

8. *Casting too high or too low.* First ensure that your line entries are narrow, both behind and in front. Then correct your arcs of power, by adjusting them forward slightly to give your back cast more lift and to bring your forward cast down, or backward slightly to achieve the opposite effects. Under most circumstances the line should extend horizontally.

9. *Failure to follow through after the forward cast.*

10. *"Hooking" or "Slicing."* Avoid any tendency to swing the rod to either side of its plane of movement. Once a cast has been made, you cannot alter its direction.

11. *Leader fouling up in the air.* An excessively narrow entry can cause this, and the remedy is to widen your entries by increasing your arcs of power and following through properly. Another possible cause is a leader which is too fine.

12. *Line or fly fouling the rod or striking your head.* If there is a cross wind from the right while you

are casting right-handed, change to left-handed casting, or vice versa. Avoid jerky movements.

As soon as you have mastered the mechanics of the overhead cast to your satisfaction you will want to learn how to lengthen and control your line. Strip a few feet of line from the reel with your left hand, still using your right forefinger to prevent the slack line from running out through the guides. Make an overhead cast, releasing your forefinger soon after the forward power arc has been completed and early in the follow through, while the line is extending in the air in front. If your shoot has been timed perfectly, the line will run out smoothly and easily. If it travels out with a jerky rasp, the shoot is too early; it must be carried out while the line is extending forwards. If the line fails to shoot, it may be because you are releasing it too late, or putting insufficient drive into your casts. The period of maximum drive should be very brief with a short line, most of the arc of power being devoted to acceleration and deceleration.

As a prelude to your next cast, draw in some line through the guides with your left hand, catching it with your right forefinger, and hold the slack in loose coils between your left forefinger and thumb. Make your overhead cast, shooting the line from the coils by allowing them to run from your left hand at the same time as you free the line from your right forefinger. Practice this until you achieve correct timing and co-ordination.

Try adding another few feet of line to your cast by stripping it from the reel, then withdrawing line through the guides and holding the coils as before, as you make your cast and shoot. Soon you should be able to manage casts of seventy-five feet, withdrawing and shooting line at each cast. The withdrawal of line against the flow of a fast river is a great aid to a clean pick up.

So far all your casts have been made in a downstream direction; now you will have to learn to place the fly across the river after fishing it down. In order to change direction, withdraw line and pick up as usual, but make your forward cast outwards to your right side (casting right handed) without shooting any line; let your line extend fully, but before it can touch the water make a second back cast and repeat the outward forward cast, this time shooting line and following through (Fig. 61).

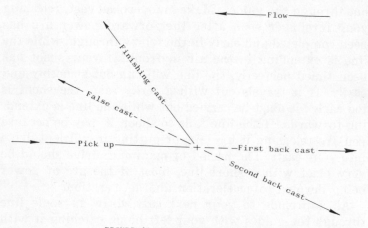

FIGURE 61. Changing direction.

Instead of waiting for the current to swing your line and fly downstream as you would ordinarily fish out a cast, you can save time while learning by roll casting it downstream right-handed. If there is sufficient space you can change hands and use the overhead cast so that your downstream casts are teaching you to cast left-handed and your casts across the river are teaching you to cast right-handed. Possibly by the time you have changed hands and made your left-handed pick up the flow will have carried your line and fly far enough downstream to enable you to change direction without an intermediate false cast; so practice also with the river flowing from left to right, which is the normal situation for casting left-handed.

Practice assiduously through all the stages of learning the overhead swing cast both left-handed and right-handed with your sunk fly and greased line outfits, but limit your distance always to the length of line you can handle properly. Concentrate on your style, which should be relaxed and easy, as though you were swinging an axe. Gradually your maximum distance will increase to perhaps ninety feet, but don't rush for distance, and don't force your rods, particularly your greased line rod. On the other hand it is important to be able to cast a fairly long line because the sunk fly fishes best at the end of a long line, covers more water and therefore takes more fish. Limit your sessions to about an hour at a time and make them as frequent as possible.

The Vertical Overhead Cast

A very powerful cast, the vertical overhead cast is achieved by bending the body instead of swinging the shoulders. Although it is done in a vertical plane, ambidexterity is important, for whenever possible it is advisable to place one's feet more or less upstream and downstream from each other, particularly while wading. However, since in casting right-handed the right foot should be forward and vice versa, it will be found that in fishing from the left bank of a river (with the current flowing from right to left) a left-handed casting position will have to be assumed in order to maintain the proper foothold. Similarly, for fishing from the right bank, a right-handed casting position is correct.

Since this cast's chief characteristic is its power, best results will be obtained by using a powerful rod, and I suggest that your sunk fly outfit should bear the main brunt of this lesson. When you have attained a reasonable standard of proficiency, by all means take out your greased line tackle and see what it will do for you, but remember that it is more delicate and sensitive, so treat it accordingly. It would be wise to wear a hat; you will be surprised at the violent impact inflicted by the line or fly (even a wet wool tag) as the result of a casting error.

With the flow from left to right, begin by laying out fifty feet of line downstream with the overhead swing cast (left-handed). Now adjust to the right-handed vertical overhead casting position by reversing your hold of the rod, but let your feet remain as they are, the right foot being downstream from the left. Pull in about ten feet of line with your left hand, holding it in loose coils, at the same time securing the line against the top of the grip with your right forefinger; simultaneously raise your rod to forty-five degrees in the first phase.

In the second phase hold the butt close to the centre of your body while your right hand throws the rod up vertically so that it comes to rest in front of your face, at the same time bending your body backwards slightly and rocking your balance on to your left foot. Pause for the line to straighten behind you (Fig. 62). In the third phase, bend forwards slightly from the hips as you force your right arm forwards to its full extent. Continue into the fourth phase by raising your left hand slightly and rocking forwards on to your right foot as the line extends, shooting the coils of slack line from your left hand when the entry is about half-way forward (Fig. 63). The timing is precisely the same as for the overhead swing cast,

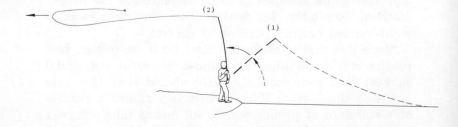

FIGURE 62. The back cast.

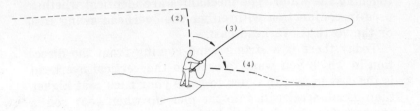

FIGURE 63. The forward cast.

an even count for all of the four phases, which should be blended smoothly.

Using the roll pick up whenever necessary, practice withdrawing and shooting line at every cast; then change direction with a false cast between your pick up and final cast. Lengthen line gradually, mastering each additional length before increasing your distance further. Adjust your arcs of power to obtain narrow entries. Practice right-handed and left-handed. With a strong fourteen-foot rod and a sunk fly line you may soon be reaching out to a hundred feet or more, but with your greased line outfit you should be satisfied with casts of eighty to ninety feet.

The Wind Cast

When performed with a salmon fly rod, the wind cast is merely a slight variation of the overhead casts. If the wind is from the left, cast right-handed over the right shoulder, and vice versa. If the wind is dead against you or only slightly to one side, use the vertical overhead. A wind from behind you is ideal for the Spey cast, which will be explained in a later section.

There are two main objectives in casting against or across a strong wind. The first is to make a high back cast so that the forward cast will be low, and the second is to slam the line out fast so that it extends fully before touching the water. The mechanics are identical whether used in conjunction with either the overhead swing cast or the vertical overhead cast.

Today there is a strong wind coming from the direction in which you want to cast, so the vertical overhead is the cast to use. In order to raise your back cast higher than usual, accelerate into the pick up when your rod is at about ten o'clock instead of ten-thirty. While you lift the rod into the vertical position (second phase) raise the butt with your left hand (if you are casting right-handed) and reach up with your right, still keeping the butt close to your body (Fig. 64). During the pause when your line

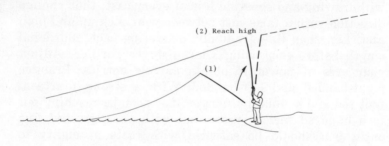

FIGURE 64. The back cast.

is extending high behind you, lower your hands into the normal position for starting your vertical overhead forward cast. In the third phase, bend forwards slightly throwing your right arm forwards to its full extent, at the same time bending your left elbow sharply so that your left hand whips the butt up against the front of your right armpit (Fig. 65). This will "point" the rod and cause the line to travel very fast and low over the water, but if carried out correctly it will be possible to shoot as much line as is required. The fourth phase, which is the follow through, may be finished more quickly than usual.

The action in the third phase could be compared to that

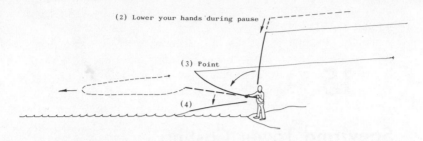

(2) Lower your hands during pause

(3) Point

(4)

FIGURE 65. The forward cast.

of bringing a shotgun up to the shoulder for a quick shot. It is, of course, essential that the line should form a narrow entry in the forward cast in order to cut through the wind. The wind cast does not apply to the routine of changing direction by means of a false cast, the principles being applied only to the final cast.

The wind cast is not really complicated, and is less energetic than it appears on paper. It differs from the overhead casts only in the high back cast and the quick "point." A little practice will make it seem simple.

15

Spey and Tower Casting

The Spey Cast

The single Spey cast may be used for all occasions except against a strong wind or across a downstream wind, or from a high bank. For a downstream wind the double Spey cast is to be used.

While the Spey cast originated on the River Spey in Scotland, there is no reason at all why it should not be used for fishing any other river with a fly, for it possesses a number of features which can be put to very good use. It has already been pointed out that the overhead cast requires a lot of space for the back cast; the fly never goes behind the angler during the Spey cast, therefore it is ideal for fishing pools when there are obstructions behind. Since the Spey cast is designed for picking a line up from downstream and casting it across, it is an efficient method of fly-fishing a river. When the wind is from behind or either side, a common occurrence with the overhead cast is a "whip-crack" signifying that the fly has gone, and knots often form in the leader; but these problems are eliminated in the Spey cast which is assisted by a wind from behind or either side (if we include the double Spey cast). With the Spey cast there is no fear of breaking a hook on the rocks behind, or of the fly getting hung up on a bush or long grass in the back cast. Furthermore, almost as long a line can be cast with the Spey cast as with the overhead cast.

There is, however, one drawback to Spey casting. It imposes severe torsion on fly rods, which will in time break down near the ferrules, unless, as mentioned earlier, they are specially built to withstand such stresses or are spliced.

For this reason your rod for Spey casting must fall within these two categories, and only on rare occasions or for short periods should an ordinary ferrule-jointed rod be subjected to Spey casting.

Conditions for learning and practicing the Spey cast are similar to those for learning the roll cast. Therefore, if it is at all possible, find a fast shallow river in which you can wade or stand on a gravel bar. Spey casting should be learned both right-handed and left-handed, so choose a place to cast right-handed where the flow is from your right to your left, and left-handed where the flow is from your left to your right. Casting from a high bank is out of the question. Your tackle should comprise your sunk fly outfit.

Assuming that your first casting session will be right-handed, stand facing across the river and slightly downstream with your feet comfortably apart, the left foot a little towards your own bank. Curl your left hand around the butt, and hold the grip with your right hand near the top. Lay out about fifty feet of line downstream with the overhead cast or roll cast.

The Spey cast is performed in four phases, the last three phases in equal timing. First, withdraw a few feet of line with the left hand while you raise the rod tip slightly to surface the line against the pull of the current. Holding the loop of spare line with your right forefinger, in the second phase continue raising the rod to an angle of about sixty degrees, which, if done properly, should bring all except the leader and fly to the surface (Fig. 68). If it fails to do so, make a roll cast and raise the rod again. In the third phase swing your body and rod to the right, allowing the rod tip to dip in the middle of its arc. This should lift the line just clear of the water throwing it outwards by centrifugal force in such a manner that the leader and fly will pitch on to the surface in front of you while the belly of the line forms a "D" behind the rod (Figs. 66, 67 and 69). The swing of the rod is contin-

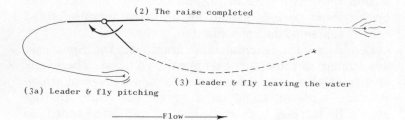

(2) The raise completed

(3a) Leader & fly pitching   (3) Leader & fly leaving the water

————Flow———▸

FIGURE 66. Plan of the Spey cast.

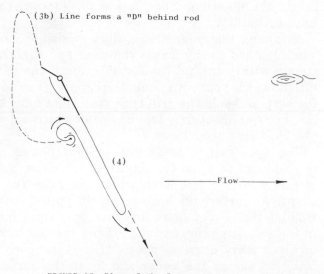

(3b) Line forms a "D" behind rod

(4)

————Flow———▸

FIGURE 67. Plan of the Spey cast.

FIGURE 68. The raise completed.

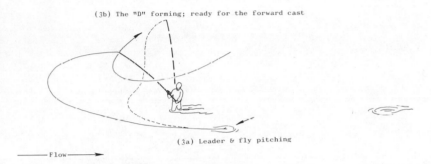

FIGURE 69. The swing.

ued so that your right hand comes to rest close to your shoulder in preparation for the forward cast. In the fourth phase, swing your body a little to the left and at the same time throw your right arm outwards to its full extent in a forty-five degree direction across and downstream, driving the rod forwards in a nearly vertical plane, and shooting the slack line a little before the rod finishes its downward movement in the forward cast (Figs. 67, 70 and 71). When the Spey cast is done properly the line, leader and fly should sail out straight and true without thrashing the water. Timing for the second, third and fourth phases is an even "one-two-three, one-two-three, one-two-three" (slow waltz time). As for all casting, the movements of the Spey cast should be smoothly blended together into a rhythm free from hesitation and jerks.

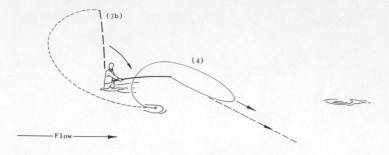

FIGURE 70. The forward cast.

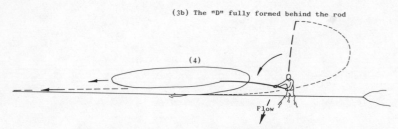

FIGURE 71. The forward cast (viewed from downstream).

When you have completed a Spey cast, to save time pick up and place the fly downstream by means of an overhead cast, or a roll pick-up and overhead cast, preparatory to making another Spey cast.

You are likely to experience difficulties at first in timing the first and second phases so that only the leader and fly are in the water as you swing into the third phase; in pitching the leader and fly to the surface in the correct spot during the third phase; in achieving a satisfactory loop, or "D" of line behind the rod; and in timing the "shoot" to pull out all your slack line smoothly in the forward cast. All these difficulties can be overcome with practice, and with experience exact manipulation will become instinctive. The placing of the leader and fly in the third phase is achieved partly by the power of the swing and partly by the dip of the rod tip, and you will find in practice that there is no need to wait any longer than is necessary for the fly and leader to touch the surface of the water, for they will settle as the rod is brought into the vertical position ready for the forward cast. The proper place for the leader and fly to pitch is in front of you, but just out of the way of your forward cast. If it is in the way, your forward cast will cross your leader and foul it; if it has been swung too far upstream, the belly of the line will fail to form an adequate "D," so your forward cast will lose power and control. Shooting the line depends on the power of the cast and perfect timing, which only trial and error can teach you.

When you have mastered the Spey cast with a short line, strip a few more feet of line from your reel, arrange it in loose coils in your left hand, and add a further coil or two to it as you pull in line from downstream in the first phase of your next cast. Try to shoot all this line, and continue to practice with the extra length. Keep on persevering with increasing lengths of line, practicing with each length until you can handle it confidently before attempting to progress further. When you can reach out to eighty or ninety feet you are doing well. Alternate your sessions between right-handed and left-handed casting until you are proficient in both. Remember to hold the rod butt close to your body, to swing the rod in a dipping sideways movement in the third phase, and to make your forward cast in a nearly vertical plane, somewhat similar to an overhead forward cast.

The Double Spey Cast

As mentioned earlier, when there is a downstream wind the single Spey cast cannot be used, because the wind will blow the line against the angler before the forward cast can be completed. But the double Spey was de-

Thirty-four Ways to Cast a Fly

signed for casting across a downstream wind, and it retains the characteristics and efficiency of the single Spey.

There are two major differences between the single Spey and the double Spey. First, the positions of your hands (but not of your feet) are reversed, so that you will be casting left-handed from the left side of a river and right-handed from the right side; and secondly, an additional movement is incorporated between the third and fourth phases of the single Spey to transform it into a double Spey cast. The rest of the double Spey is similar to the single Spey cast.

Assuming you will at first be casting left-handed, the water will be flowing from right to left as you face the opposite bank. Begin by laying out fifty feet of line downstream. Now move your left foot a little further forward than for the single Spey, so that it is more or less directly downstream from your right foot, and hold the rod left-handed, your right hand at the butt and your left near the top of the grip.

In the first phase, withdraw line with the right hand and bring the line to the surface against the pull of the current, roll casting if necessary. In the second phase, raise the rod to a sixty degree angle. Continue into the third phase by swinging to the right and bringing your left hand across your body so that the rod makes the same sideways arc as in the third phase of the single Spey, but without approaching the vertical position, and the fly pitches approximately in the same place. Now swing left in the fourth phase, continuing the arc in precisely the same manner as in the single Spey until your rod is nearly vertical, but taking care to leave the fly undisturbed where it was pitched. The downstream wind will help this movement. By now the belly of the line should have formed a "D" behind your rod, ready for the near-vertical forward cast across and down river, which is the fifth phase; so complete your forward cast as in the single

Spey, shooting the slack line. Timing is equal for all the last four phases, slow waltz time (please refer to Figures 72 to 75). Provided you can accomplish the single Spey cast proficiently you should have no trouble in mastering the double Spey.

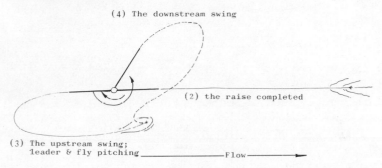

FIGURE 72. Plan of the double Spey cast.

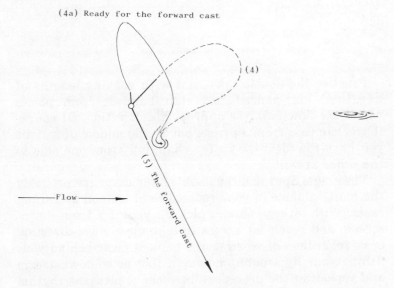

FIGURE 73. Plan of the double Spey cast.

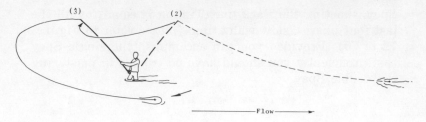

FIGURE 74.   The upstream swing.

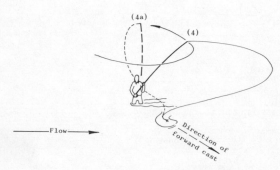

FIGURE 75. The downstream swing.

Practice the double Spey cast with varying lengths of
line, both left-handed and right-handed, from places
where the flow is in the appropriate direction. Of course
if you can cast from a gravel bar in the middle of a river
you have the ideal set-up for changing from one side to
the other at will.

The single Spey and the double Spey casts are probably
the most valuable in your repertoire of salmon fly fishing
casts. With either you can pick up your fly from downstream and reach far across in a single change-direction
cast, regardless of whether the bank is clear behind you;
fishing your fly around, moving a foot or so downstream
and repeating the procedure becomes a pleasant rhythm
in itself, as you cover a stretch of river thoroughly and
efficiently.

The Tower Cast

Although the tower (or steeple) cast is derived from the overhead cast, I think it would be appropriate to group it with the Spey casts by reason of the conditions governing its use. It has been said that the Spey cast is extremely difficult to perform from a high bank; the tower cast is very easy to perform from such an eminence, and since the line and fly are thrown above the angler's head instead of behind him as in the overhead cast, the tower cast makes it possible to fish even a canyon where no other cast would be feasible. Its chief limitation is that only a relatively short line can be cast.

The tower cast can be accomplished equally successfully with either your greased line or sunk fly outfit, and should be practiced both right-handed and left-handed. Since a high bank facilitates the tower cast, a suitable location should be selected.

Begin with about thirty feet of line. If you are fishing on the left bank, with the flow from right to left stand with your right foot towards where you intend to cast and hold the rod for casting right-handed, with the butt as low as possible.

In the first phase, raise the rod to forty-five degrees. If this fails to surface nearly all the line, shorten it by pulling in the required amount of line with your left hand, catching it with your right forefinger. Most of the line should now be below the rod tip. In the second phase, lift the rod upwards as high as you can reach, maintaining the forty-five degrees angle; this will propel the line upwards in the form of a question mark (Fig. 76). Immediately the lift has been completed, and while the line and fly are travelling upwards, move the rod into the vertical overhead cast position (Fig. 77). In the third phase, make a vertical overhead forward cast or a high wind cast, depending on circumstances. In the fourth phase, shoot line and follow through so that your rod tip stops close enough to the water to prevent retraction of the

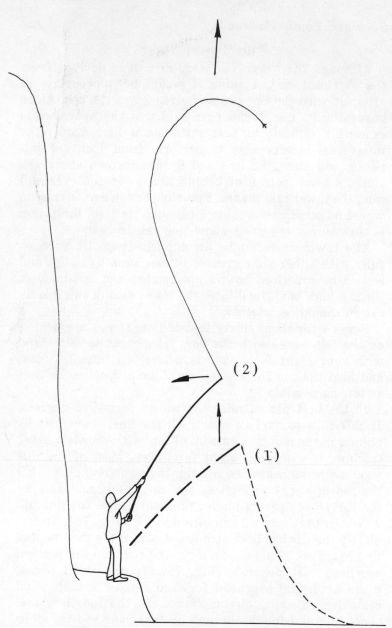

FIGURE 76. Lifting the line.

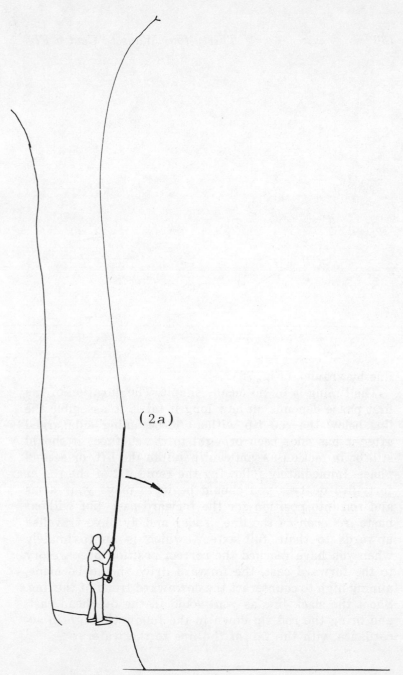

(2a)

FIGURE 77. Ready for the forward cast.

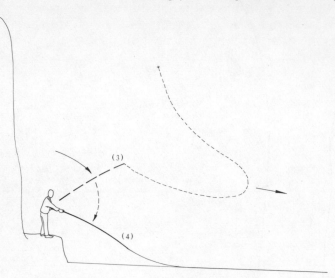

FIGURE 78. The forward cast and the low follow through.

line by gravity (Fig. 78).

The timing is by no means simple. The duration of the first phase depends on how long it takes to assemble the line below the rod tip without it becoming submerged after it has once been brought to the surface; it should still be in motion as you continue into the lift, or second phase. Immediately following the rapid lift of the rod at forty-five degrees you should begin to move your arms and rod into position for the forward cast, but without haste. As soon as the line, leader and fly have travelled upwards to their full extent, which is approximately when you have reached the correct position preparatory to the forward cast, the forward drive should be made, aiming high to counteract the downward trend of the line. Shoot the slack line as you would in the overhead cast, and bring the rod tip down in the follow through in accordance with the fall of the line to the water.

Practice with increasing lengths of line, right-handed and left-handed, shooting as much line as you can. Your maximum distance may be only about sixty feet, but the tower cast will enable you to fish your fly in some very productive waters which might otherwise be passed by.

16

Casting and Mending a Slack Line

The techniques explained in this chapter may sometimes be of value in fishing the sunk fly. For example, it may be necessary to cast a slack line, perhaps well upstream of the best holding water, in order to sink the fly deeply enough to fish it properly; or the line may have to be "mended" once immediately after a cast has been made and before it has had time to sink in order to start the fly on its prescribed course. They are, however, the very essence of greased line fishing, one of whose principles is to present the fly broadside on to the fish without allowing the currents to exert unnatural drag.

Your tackle should therefore comprise your greased line rod, reel and line and a medium leader with a small woollen tag. If you have an EBg line, have the "g" or fine end next to the leader. Make sure that the line will float by rubbing it down thoroughly with one of the approved dressings (please refer to the section devoted to lines in Chapter 12), unless it is one of the lines that are specially designed to float. Leave about six feet of line at the tip "ungreased," since you want your fly to fish just under the surface. I have always found it best to "grease" the line a day or two before its use, so that the dressing has plenty of time to set.

Casting a Slack Line

It is a curious fact that a beginner experiences great difficulty in casting anything but a slack line while he is endeavoring to make it go out straight, yet when he has achieved casting proficiency he has to learn how to cast a slack line.

There are two efficient methods of obtaining the desired results with the salmon fly rod, each producing its own effects, so which method you will use depends on the circumstances. The cast which is easiest to perform in conjunction with either of these methods is the overhead cast.

The first method is to make your overhead forward cast high in the air, which will cause the leader and line to fall on the water in a close zig-zag pattern (Fig. 79). It will be obvious that a longer line needs to be cast to reach an objective with a slack line than with a straight line. The amount of slack line is governed by the upward angle of the forward cast, and to accomplish this your arcs of power for both the back cast and the forward cast must be adjusted slightly backwards, throwing the back cast low and the forward cast high. This method is excellent provided there is no wind interference, and no obstruction behind you.

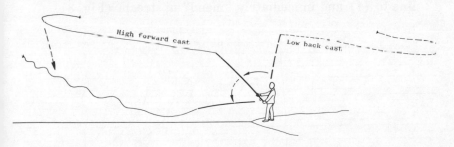

FIGURE 79. Casting a slack line (first method).

To cast a slack line by the second method, make a more powerful overhead cast than would normally be required for the length of line you are using; check your rod before following through so that the line reaches its full extent and springs back in a series of irregular waves (Fig. 80). Limit your shoot, because if you shoot too much line it will fail to spring back.

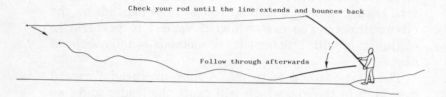

FIGURE 80. Casting a slack line (second method).

"Mending" the Line

To study the effects of the currents upon your line, it is most important that "mending" be carried out on a river. Typical situations which would cause drag are illustrated in Figures 81 and 82. In downstream drag the fast current carries your line downstream in a loop which drags the leader and fly after it very rapidly. To counteract this action of the current upon your line, cast a slack line to (1) and immediately "mend" upstream (Fig. 81).

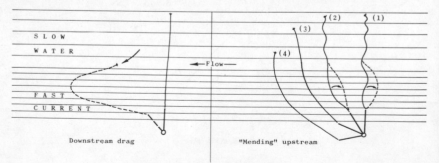

FIGURE 81. Correcting downstream drag.

By the time the fly has drifted to (2), a belly will have begun to form in the line and it must be "mended" upstream again. Allow the fly to fish through (3) and (4), leading with the rod. It will be found that as the line swings downstream each "mended" loop travels outwards towards the fly, diminishing in extent.

"Mending" the line is accomplished in this instance by lifting part of it off the surface and throwing a loop upstream. This is done by reaching out with the rod and springing the butt with the lower hand so that the tip arches over lightly. It must be carried out with a gentle sweeping movement, not violently. With a little practice you will be able to gauge the exact amount of movement required to lift and swing over the length of line to be "mended" without interfering with the drift of the fly. Care must be taken to prevent the belly of the line from becoming too pronounced before it is "mended."

To overcome upstream drag (Fig. 82), cast a slack line to (1), immediately "mending" downstream; drift the fly to (2) where the line is beginning to form a belly, and "mend" again; the fly may then be fished through (3), leading with the rod as it swings around.

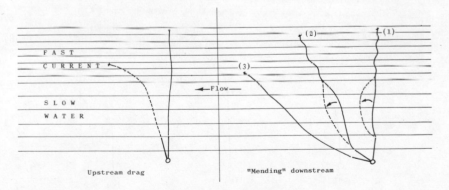

FIGURE 82. Correcting upstream drag.

Casting a "Mended" Line

Sometimes it is an advantage to be able to cast a "mended" line on to the water. This maneuver will not only save having to make the first "mend," but is also extremely valuable when a major part of the line needs to be "mended" (Fig. 84), or when a "mend" has to be placed in the line near the fly (Figs. 85 and 86).

With the vertical overhead cast it is quite easy to cast a "mended" line. If you want to cast a "mend" to the right, during the forward cast wave your rod to the right and return it to its original plane. To cast a "mend" to the left, wave your rod to the left and return to center. An early wave and return will place a "mend" close to the fly (Fig. 83–b), and a late wave and return will place it close to the rod (Fig. 83–c). To cast a big "mend" (Fig. 83–a), an early wave and a late return will be required. At first you may find it difficult to obtain anything except a "mend" near the rod; however, as your wave timing speeds up you will be able to adjust your "mends" very accurately in the air.

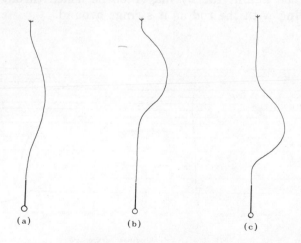

(a)   (b)   (c)

FIGURE 83. Casting a "mended" line.

When you want to drift your fly in the edge of a fast current, on the other side of a wide band of slow water (Fig. 84), cast a line with a big downstream "mend" to (1), allow the fly to drift to (2) and "mend" downstream, then fish through (3).

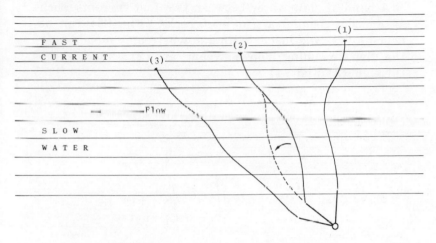

FIGURE 84. "Mending" through slow water.

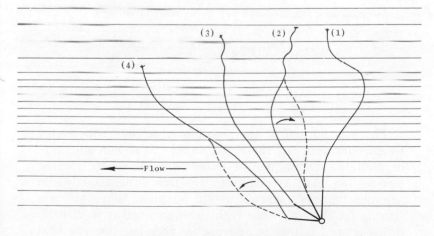

FIGURE 85. Crossing a band of fast current.

To negotiate a fast riffle between two bodies of slow water (Fig. 85), cast to (1) with an upstream "mend" close to the fly, "mend" upstream at (2), fish through (3) and make a short downstream "mend" at (4), throwing some extra line on the water as you do so.

A band of slow water between two fast currents, such as an eddy behind a group of rocks (Fig. 86) can be fished by casting to (1) with a downstream "mend" near the fly, "mending" downstream at (2), and fishing through (3) and (4).

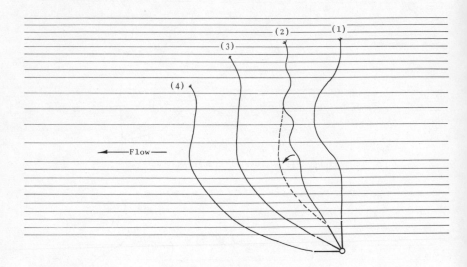

FIGURE 86. Crossing a band of slow water.

There is no end to the possible situations which may be encountered, but these few examples should suffice to explain the techniques of overcoming drag in greased line fishing. Avoid "mending" the line unnecessarily; let all your "mends" serve a useful purpose. When you are fishing let the fly swing right around until it is directly downstream, but as it approaches this position see that the rod tip is held up, so that if a fish takes at this critical moment, as is likely to happen, you will be able to give line. Then as you begin to retrieve line in preparation for your next cast, pull in the first few feet slowly and deliberately, because a fish which has followed your fly around will probably seize it as it starts to move upstream.

Post Script

     Since writing the foregoing, certain radical changes have occurred in the realm of fly fishing tackle. I am greatly impressed by the revolutionary improvements in glass rods as well as the addition of new fly lines which have been expressly designed for special uses. I therefore feel bound to explain some of these changes.

     Good bamboo for built cane rods has become very scarce indeed, and this has had a stimulating effect on the manufacture of rods from synthetic materials. So much so that glass rods are now being used extensively for tournament casting, where success can only be achieved with the finest products available.

     Although I still prefer the cane rods in my possession, I have in the past few months had occasion to handle two rods made by the same manufacturer, and as the result have felt obliged to revise my previous thoughts about glass rods. Both these rods had very pleasing actions, they were comparable to the best cane rods, and they delighted their independent and widely separated owners, who had taken many fish with them and were experienced fly fishermen with a thorough knowledge of glass and cane fly rods. Both were Fenwick 9-ft., 4⅝ ozs. rods, and were designated respectively FF-90 and FF-98. The former is a light quick-action fly rod, but the one I handled had already overcome trout up to eight pounds; the latter is a very powerful rod capable of casting a long line under adverse conditions and of subduing steelhead and salmon.

     Now that their teething troubles appear to be over, glass rods will probably continue to improve, and may be on the way to superseding cane in the same way that cane superseded greenheart.

     Fly lines that have been developed recently include the

Scientific Angler Wet Head, which permits mending and control although the fly can be fished deep; this is especially useful for steelhead fishing, but would no doubt be equally effective for other fishing when control of a sunk fly by greased line techniques would be desirable. New improvements in forward-taper or "torpedo-head" lines for reaching out easily have also been introduced lately.

I have referred specifically to several Hardy products in my remarks concerning salmon fly tackle. However, since the time of writing the firm of Hardy Brothers Limited has been acquired by Messrs. Harris and Sheldon. Such a transaction could of course lead to new policies which might affect some of the items mentioned.

A new system for classifying fly lines has recently been adopted for general use. This is the AFTMA code, based on line weights.

With the advent of new materials and modern methods of manufacture, lines of the same thickness may vary somewhat in weight, thus presenting some difficulty in the choice of a line which will balance a certain rod correctly. The differences in weights are particularly noticeable in the comparison of floating and sinking lines of the same diameters.

The AFTMA code is designed as an aid in the selection of the correct line for your fly rod. The following examples will indicate how the code works: DT7F denotes a double-taper, weight #7, floating line; WF8S denotes a weight-forward (forward taper), weight #8, sinking line; WF9FS denotes a weight-forward, weight #9, floating line with a sinking tip; and DT6I denotes a double-taper, weight #6, intermediate line (one that can be made to float or sink, such as a silk line). The most suitable weight of line to balance an all-purpose fly rod which is 8' 9" long and weighs around 5¼ ozs. would probably be #7. However, most of the better quality rods now have the recommended AFTMA line-weight code numbers marked on them, and they should be adhered to.

Index to Trout Fly Casting

Index to Salmon Fly Casting